Volume 24

understanding
human behavior

An Illustrated Guide to Successful Human Relationships

✕ COLUMBIA HOUSE / New York

Editor	Nicolas Wright
Deputy Editor	Susan Joiner
Senior Designer	Stewart Cowley
Art Editor	Mary Cooper
Art Assistant	Jeff Gurney
Editorial Assistants	Mundy Ellis
	Sarie Forster
	John Moore
	Michael McIntyre
Picture Research	Diane Rich
	Hazel Robinson
	Paul Snelgrove
Editorial Director	Graham Donaldson
Production Manager	Warren E. Bright

contents

introduction

We all need somebody to love, but how did you go about finding a mate? Some give their vital statistics to a computer and expect a perfect match, some go to marriage bureaus in the hope of finding a life partner, and others advertise their particulars in the personal columns and await a suitable response. Volume Twenty-four of *Understanding Human Behavior* investigates the match-making business. But in their quest for love some are left with nothing but memories. What went wrong, and can it be righted next time? Volume Twenty-four also discusses how to end an affair.

How much do you rely on other people? That answer may lie in your upbringing. Volume Twenty-four asks how children come to leave their parents and how they then adjust to society, often experimenting with alternative ways of living. One crucial aspect of these new life-styles is the way they challenge established rules. Is authority losing its grip today? In this volume, we dissect the structure of authority and examine the possibility of it breaking down. There is also a report on the criminal who is always caught by the tell-tale traces he leaves behind at the scene of the crime.

Who rules the national roost? Usually it is the politician and sometimes he is entirely the wrong

(continued)

person for the job. Volume Twenty-four analyzes the political animal, along with the PR man he sometimes hires to put across his image to the public. This volume asks if politicians and PR men are really necessary. It also studies the evolution of man and asks whether he will become a superman — or simply become extinct. And there is a report on what has been described as "future shock" — the confusion and disorientation we are experiencing because of the rapid rate of change — and what we can do about it.

Volume Twenty-four uncovers the fact that just about every occupation has a health risk of some kind. And it also looks at that unmentionable disease, cancer, and our efforts to understand and treat it. How insecure are you? The Self-Improvement series helps you determine your ability to cope with insecurity and also teaches you to say goodbye in a constructive and creative way. The series also features a test which gives you an idea of just how good you are at achieving your goals. Finally, Volume Twenty-four includes an indispensable, comprehensive index which gives you access to information in any volume.

—The Editor

Alan Lee

Occupational hazard

Tinker, tailor or candlestick maker, each runs the risk of watching his pals go by.

When the phrase "occupational diseases" is mentioned people tend to think in terms of the manual trades. We have known for centuries, for example, about the havoc that coal dust can wreak in miners' lungs. We are familiar with the fact that those in the chemical and metal industries can be poisoned by the substances they work with. We have been aware that painters, potters, glassblowers, agricultural workers—to name but a few—are all at a special kind of risk.

But it is now clear that just about every job, whether manual, clerical, or even professional, carries with it an increased risk of disease.

Your dentist, for example, used to spend his working day standing in awkward positions. So nearly half of all dentists complain of backache, compared with about one person in ten in the rest of the population. Six in ten of them have some sort of defor-

mity, like unbalanced bodies due to the postures they have to adopt. And a quarter of them have flat feet.

Of course, many dentists today have sophisticated equipment which enables them to sit down at their work, but nonetheless recent statistics in Britain, for example, showed that more dentists died in the 45–54 age group than in any other profession.

The executive works under physical and mental stress—a fact which has

Protective Clothing

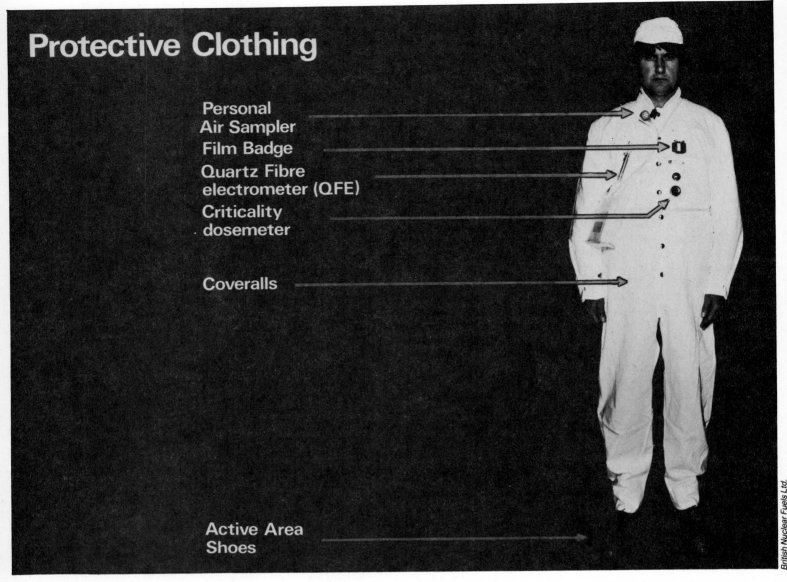

Personal
Air Sampler

Film Badge

Quartz Fibre
electrometer (QFE)

Criticality
dosemeter

Coveralls

Active Area
Shoes

Nuclear fuel workers guard against the hazards of their environment with a sophisticated array of protective gadgets and clothes.

been explored and well-documented in recent years—so this is another job which can promote ill health.

And even writers and newsmen are not immune—they tend to drink too much, smoke too much, and sit down too much, all of which puts their health at greater-than-average risk.

The growing awareness that all sorts of jobs can create specific problems has led to an expansion in the branch of medicine concerned with the study of occupational disease.

The most obvious problems, however, do still occur in the manual and manufacturing trades, but here too there has been a major revolution in recent decades both in health and safety legislation, in compulsory protective measures, and in compensation for those afflicted because of the jobs they do.

Nonetheless too many workers are still being crippled, or even killed, because of their jobs, and much remains to be done to make our places of work safer and healthier.

It seems that Paracelsus, in the sixteenth century, was the first physician to recognize that certain trades caused disease. He described the chronic inflammation in the lungs of miners and noted the way smelters were poisoned by heavy metals.

The first really systematic study of occupational disease, however, was done by the Italian physician Bernardino Ramazzini, who in 1700 published a book called *Diseases of Workers*. He called attention to such conditions as stonemasons' and miners' pneumoconiosis, a lung disease caused by dust. He wrote of the vertigo and sciatica suffered by potters, and the eye troubles of gilders, painters and those in other professions who do intricate work in poor light. Ramazzini suggested, among other things, that more attention be paid to

cleanliness, adequate ventilation and better posture.

To the questions that physicians since Hippocrates have been asking the patient, he added a vital one that every doctor should ask today: "What is your job?"

And he made a telling moral point: "It is but a poor profit which is achieved by destroying health."

After Ramazzini, the situation became worse instead of better. At least in his day only a small proportion of the working population were in jobs which seriously affected their health. Many of those at risk, such as smelters, worked out in the open air which kept exposure levels down.

With the beginning of the Industrial Revolution some two centuries ago, however, there was a mass exodus from the countryside to the rapidly expanding towns. Not only were living conditions abysmal but the industrial barons who owned the new "manufactories" put profit and production far above concern about the health of their workers. The mine owners, the mill owners, the steelworks kings, the railroad entrepreneurs more often than not scarcely regarded as human those who toiled for them. Industrial diseases reached epidemic proportions.

There were those who tried to overcome the problems that industrialization created. One was Charles Turner Thakrah, a British surgeon and druggist, whose work inspired legislation to protect the health of workers.

Substantial Dangers

Most modern industries have developed techniques and equipment which greatly reduce or even eliminate health hazards, but many dangers still remain. And new processes, particularly in the chemical, metal and plastics industries, have brought with them fresh risks. Indeed almost every other day, it seems, some new substance is found to be potentially dangerous.

All in all, the experts estimate that there are at least 2,000 diseases which could be attributed to an individual's occupation, although not all are permanently crippling.

Perhaps the greatest problems throughout the ages have been created by metals, both during mining and refining and in subsequent use in industrial processes. Lead, for example, is widely used throughout industry, and lead poisoning—which can lead to paralysis, blindness, delirium and even insanity—has been a major difficulty. The occupations most at risk are plumbing and soldering, shipbreaking, printing, pottery, battery manufacture, and painting.

Many of the hazards have been all but eliminated through tough legislation and frequent medical checks for lead workers. Paints, for example, are now almost all lead-free, and the lead glazes used by potters are strictly controlled. (Incidentally, the fall of the Roman Empire is sometimes blamed on insidious lead poisoning. Water was carried in lead pipes, cooking pots had lead glazes, and this, it is said, led to sterility, miscarriages, stillbirths, and other troubles among the Roman ruling classes.)

Masks, gloves and respirators are now extensively used in the lead trades as are strong ventilation systems to remove dust, fumes and toxic gases. But there have been occasional outbreaks, notably in the early years of the car industry when tetraethyl lead was used as a degreasing agent.

Mercury can produce problems for its miners and refiners, for thermom-

G. R. Roberts

eter manufacturers and, the classic case, for those working in the felt hat industry. Mercuric nitrate was used to bind the felt, and the workers often developed "hatter's shakes"—a tremor starting in the fingers and progressing to other parts of the body. As well as sickness, headaches and chronic diarrhea, mercury poisoning can lead to severe mental disturbance, hence the expression "as mad as a hatter." (The Mad Hatter in *Alice in Wonderland* seems to have been an extreme case.) Modern precautions, similar to those in the lead industry, have all but eliminated such problems.

Phossy Jaw

Among the other dangerous metals are manganese, cadmium and chrome. But it was a nonmetallic element, phosphorus, which caused one of the most horrifying outbreaks of industrial disease about 150 years ago. When matchmaking, using white or yellow phosphorus, began in the 1830s, many matchmakers—and they were usually women and children —developed a condition known as "phossy jaw," in which the jawbone was literally destroyed, causing terrible deformity and disfigurement.

Although the cause was identified in 1845, it took sixty years before most European countries and the United States passed legislation to ban the use of white phosphorus and substituted the safer alternatives, red phosphorus and phosphorus sesquisulphide.

Aniline, a derivative of coal tar, is used in a wide variety of industrial processes, notably dyestuffs, pharmaceutical paints, rubber processing,

Wool sorters' disease, or anthrax, is still contracted from infected hides—and it can kill.

explosives, and photographic chemicals. It can be easily absorbed through the skin, which it turns a grayish-blue color. It causes shortness of breath and, in severe cases, chronic anemia. The strictest precautions must be observed in its use.

In the late 1930s, large numbers of workers involved in rayon manufacture suddenly developed severe mental illnesses. The problem: poisoning by one of the chemicals used in the rayon-making process, carbon bisulphide. The big difficulties with this chemical are that it vaporizes at ordinary room temperatures and that breathing it in for only half an hour to an hour can be dangerous. It affects the nervous system, causing anxiety, depression and impairment of memory. Although carbon bisulphide cannot be eliminated from rayon manufacture, workers can be, and are, completely protected from it.

Skin Troubles

A common hazard to workers in many industries is dermatitis. Just about any substance can bring on skin trouble, but among the commonest villains are alkalis (notably sodas), oils, paraffin, grease, and chemicals such as drugs and detergents. Dirt and germs entering cracked skin also bring on dermatitis, and there is one substance, tar, which is extremely dangerous and can cause skin cancer.

Farm workers are at risk from skin conditions brought on by plants; building workers' skin may be attacked by cement, brick and stone dust; wood may affect the skin of furniture workers; and bakers can suffer rashes because of dough and yeast. And, of course, soaps, detergents, and cleaning materials can cause dermatitis in housewives. The hazards are now well-recognized, and barrier creams or gloves are frequently used to give protection. Cleanliness is also important.

You might think that the healthy outdoor life led by farmers and agricultural workers was free from any specific occupational risks. In fact there are several conditions peculiar to these workers. They can catch brucellosis—which in man produces a long-term debilitating illness, rather like influenza—and tetanus. Those who work with sheep or hides run the risk of anthrax, which used to be known as wool sorters' disease. The external form produces large inflamed skin swellings, accompanied by fever. The internal form results in pneumonia with hemorrhages. Today penicillin and other antibiotics can usually overcome the disease, but the internal form can still be a killer. It is, however, now rare in Europe and North America, although from time to time outbreaks occur.

One disease that has been recognized only comparatively recently is "farmer's lung," which is an allergic reaction to fungus spores in moldy hay. Symptoms are something like bronchitis. At present there is no real means of prevention, except avoidance of the irritating spores.

Sugar cane dust causes a similar lung disease called bagassosis and cotton dust and fibers cause another condition called byssinosis.

Add to these the risks of accident with agricultural machinery or being injured or killed by a toppling tractor and it can be seen that farming is by no means a safe occupation.

Deadly Dust

Looking at industrial diseases in general, one thing is clear: dust is deadly. And it is certainly deadly in the coal-mining industry. Coal dust literally clogs up a miner's lungs, first leading to a cough and shortness of breath and then possibly to bronchitis and emphysema—overinflation of the air spaces within the lungs which causes a breakdown in the thin membranes where oxygen and carbon dioxide exchange should take place.

A respiratory disease caused by dust is known as pneumoconiosis, and one of the big difficulties in preventing it is that the particles which cause most

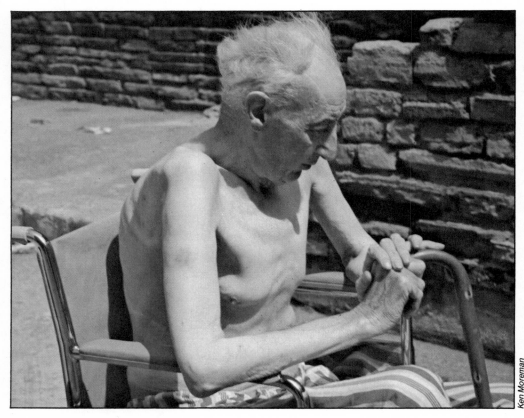

Ken Moreman

harm are invisible, ranging in size from .0002 to .005 of a millimeter. Larger particles tend to settle to the floor or are filtered out by the hairs in the breathing passages before they reach the lungs. Smaller ones are either exhaled or absorbed through the lungs into the bloodstream and eventually excreted.

The pneumoconioses are usually categorized by the offending dust. Thus coal dust causes anthracosis; fine sand or crushed rock, found in metal-casting, quarrying and pottery making, causes silicosis; and asbestos dust can produce asbestosis.

Scar Tissue

All of them produce a fibrous growth of scar tissue within the lungs, which can fuse into large masses. The disease can be complicated by tuberculosis, although this is much rarer than it used to be. Affected lungs are permanently impaired so the only course of action is either prevention of the dust at the work place or regular examination of those at risk so that they may change their jobs at the first sign of trouble. Over the years, however, respiratory diseases have affected tens of thousands of miners, crippling their health and shortening their lives considerably.

One of the classic cases of silicosis occurred at Gauley Bridge, West Virginia, in the late 1920s and early 1930s. A waterpower tunnel was being bored along the new River through

For the chair-bound chronic bronchitis sufferer, the pleasures of life are few. Inhaling deadly dust has left him forever out of breath.

sandstone and quartz rocks, which are made up almost entirely of silica. Silica dust is even more virulent than coal dust, but the thousands of workers who flocked to the site in the depression years of 1929-32 were given no protective masks.

Within three years, 500 had died of silicosis or from silica-induced pneumonia or tuberculosis. And many have undoubtedly died as a result of exposure since, because silicosis, like the other pneumoconioses, can take many years to manifest itself.

Asbestos dust can also lead to severe inflammation of the lungs, although strong ventilation in mills and processing factories has led to a considerable decline in cases over the last forty years. Nonetheless the material is in widespread use and can still cause problems. One of the worrying factors is that asbestos victims are far more likely than average to contract cancer of the lungs. As well as dust, the tiny fibers of asbestos are implicated in serious conditions, like gastrointestinal cancer.

Cancer itself is a hazard in several industries. Rubber workers, for example, are prone to bladder cancer because of exposure to the antioxidants used in its manufacture. So too are exterminators and gas workers.

Quite a few other chemicals, often complex hydrocarbons, have been identified as carcinogens—that is, substances capable of triggering off cancers. Workers who may come into contact with them should wear protective clothing and, where gases are concerned, use breathing apparatus.

Even wood dust or shavings, it seems, can be carcinogens: an investigation of furniture makers in High Wycombe in England a few years ago showed that they had a much higher than average incidence of cancers of the nose and sinus. Nickel, too, causes similar cancers, and some of the mineral oils used in metal cutting and rolling are known to cause scrotal cancer. This latter disease used to attack chimney sweeps in particular, the culprit being hydrocarbon chemicals in soot.

In all susceptible industries, it is essential that strict attention be paid to safety precautions and protective clothing, to regular checks, to high standards of cleanliness.

Radiation Sickness

A comparatively modern hazard is radiation sickness, and all those working with X-rays, radium or other radioactive substances need special protection. Built-in shielding on X-ray machines in hospitals guard staff against stray radiation. But radiologists, radiotherapists and the like still wear special radiation-counting "badges." These are regularly checked to ensure that the wearers have not received too high a dose during their work. And when X-rays are used in industry—to examine stresses in metals, for example—workers should always wear leaded aprons and gloves and watch the operation through a lead-glass screen.

One group that used to be particularly at risk from radiation disease were those who painted the dials of luminous watches. Usually young girls, they used to lick their paintbrushes to "point" them before painting the dials with radioactive zinc sulphide. The radiation attacked their mouths, teeth and eventually the whole of their bodies. Many died before they reached thirty.

These are only some of the wide variety of occupational diseases to which we are prey. Two other hazards of modern life are noise and stress—they too are killers and cripplers.

A continuous noise level of some 90 to 100 decibels is by no means uncommon in factories. That is equivalent to the noisiest motorbike revving up a few yards from your ear, and some

United Kingdom Atomic Energy Authority

workers suffer such exposure day in, day out for forty years. It is not surprising that one British survey found that those in really noisy surroundings, such as in steel mills, drop forges, nylon-spinning works and bottling plants, are 14 times more likely to have hearing loss at the end of their working lives than the average man.

Generally it is perception of the higher frequencies of sound which is affected and, while the sufferer does not usually become totally deaf, this makes understanding speech very difficult, if not impossible. There are ways of making machinery quieter, but many manufacturers say they simply cannot afford to do so. The eardrums of workers can be protected with earmuffs and plugs, but many workers do not bother to wear them.

Twitches and Tics

Mental stress at work is difficult to measure, and there are wide variations in individual response to stressful situations. Some people seem to thrive on it, but in others it can lead to mental illness, including acute depression. Twitches, tics, headaches, insomnia, stomach upsets, and skin rashes may all result from an inability to cope with the mental strains of work. So too can ulcers, heart palpitations, infertility and high blood pressure. In all such cases the doctor must tackle not only the physical symptoms, but also the

In the sealed radioactive area, workers carry their own individual atmosphere in oxygenated suits.

psychological factors, and this may mean a change of job.

Over the years the industrialized nations have gradually begun to build up a body of legislation to protect workers from occupational disease, and most recognize diseases for which compensation may be claimed. But although the worst examples of carelessness shown by early industrialists have been overcome and statutory safety precautions and protective measures have been introduced, much still remains to be done.

Living Dangerously

For example, workers must be told of the potential dangers of their jobs before they start them, and even today this does not happen enough. The need to protect themselves must be continually emphasized, for often workers shun protective clothing and apparatus even when it is available. And the price of health and safety at work is continual vigilance and regular checks of both the manufacturing processes and the mental and physical health of the workers.

There will always be dangerous jobs to do, but society owes it to the worker to make certain that the risks are kept to an absolute minimum.

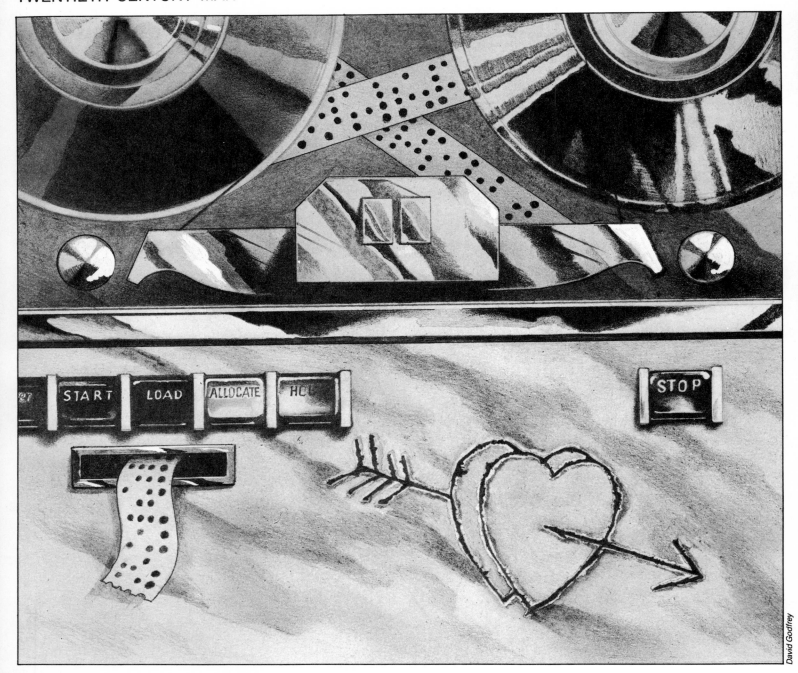

David Godfrey

Dial-a-date

In the age of technology, those who don't trust in fate rely on computers to find them a mate.

People who use agencies to find a partner of the opposite sex are popularly supposed to fit into a single stereotype: physically unattractive, shy or neurotic, with inadequate social skills, and probably past their first youth—certainly over 25. In other words, people who have difficulties in finding partners by "normal" social means must, by definition, be lacking in powers of attraction.

This might once have been largely true. The normal methods by which a young person gets to know eligible persons of the opposite sex is through a close network of family and neighbors, probably a neighborhood school, and finally going to work in local offices or factories. There is continuity in such a life-style: most of an 18-year-old's partners will have been known to him since childhood. The social and geographical mobility of our society has changed all that to a large extent, and in fact most of the people using computer dating services are ordinarily attractive and socially desirable people.

It is necessary only to consider some common users of computer dating services to realize that some perfectly eligible people are peculiarly isolated by the mobility of our society—for instance, air stewardesses and some university students.

The air stewardess is, of course, literally one of the most mobile of people: she travels constantly as part of a small crew, usually stopping no more than one night at any given stopping place. Something between a secretary and a waitress, her job is nevertheless considered a glamorous occupation. To qualify, she has to be physically presentable and pleasant-mannered and probably rather gregarious—by definition, a popular type. She is likely to have had many friends and acquaintances, but once she begins work as an airstewardess she will find it increasingly difficult to keep contact with them, let alone to form any new relationships.

The difficulties of a young man at an all-male university are different. He has little opportunity to develop interpersonal social skills with the opposite sex, particularly if he is living on campus. He has long vacations in which to meet girls, but if he spends this time at his parents' home, he may find that the girls he knew there are mostly occupied with local males—all earning a salary and so richer than he is. If he travels in his vacation, he may or may not make contact with unattached females, but these are often essentially ephemeral relationships. When he leaves university, he may know very few girls; and his social skills may also be inadequate, making him less able to begin making viable contacts than men with much lower educational status.

Business and Camping

He is more likely to use computer dating agencies after leaving university than before—partly for financial reasons. Twice as many males in the 21-25 age bracket use the agencies as do those in the 16–20 bracket. For both men and women, the peak age is 21-25; the second highest 26-30.

One English computer agency that keeps records of its clientele compiled profiles of what it calls its "peak" male and female clients. Like most customer profiles distributed to the press, they are probably more of a public relations exercise than a true picture. The male in particular is idealized, probably a stereotype designed to attract female clients to the agency. He supposedly has a university degree and is 5 feet 11 inches tall—that is, above average height and considerably above average educational standards. They describe him as a businessman, holding "right-wing views" and yet, curiously enough, with "no feeling either way for politics." He is 25 years old.

The "peak" female, according to this profile, is 22 years old and 6 inches smaller than the male at 5 feet 5 inches. She has had an education, is a nurse or secretary, and has "no interest in politics at all." She is a curious mixture: she sees herself as rather "extroverted" and more practical than intellectual, but she dislikes business and camping and describes herself as unsure with the opposite sex and fairly inexperienced sexually. She does not claim to be particularly ambitious or dominant—or generous; she is fashion-conscious and home-loving at the same time.

"Peak" males and females tend to dislike jazz and gambling, have "no feeling either way" for sport or social work but "like psychology."

Making a Move

A more scientifically designed breakdown divided agency clients into six categories: employer-managerial; professional; nonmanual (clerks, secretaries, etc.); skilled manual; unskilled manual; and a special category for students and foreigners and so on.

This breakdown showed that the greatest numbers of computer agency clients were in the second group, especially in professions like schoolteaching and librarianship. For every ten men in that group, there would be about five in the top group, another five in the nonmanual group, three in the skilled manual, one or two in the unskilled, and one or two in the last special group.

For every ten women in the second group, there were seven nonmanual (probably mostly secretaries), almost none in the skilled or unskilled manual groups, and only one in the top category—but then there are still comparatively few women in top jobs.

It is perhaps surprising that there are more men than women on the lists of computer dating agencies. Women in particular are usually surprised to learn of this. They cannot understand why men have any difficulty. A woman knows the limitations society still imposes on her intersexual behavior: if, at a friend's house or at any social gathering, she meets an unattached man to whom she is attracted, she may not suggest a further meeting. As in Victorian society, the suggestion must come from the man—the male chooses, the male makes the approach. This stricture is reinforced, of course, by the continuing convention that a man pays for a woman on social occasions, even when, as increasingly occurs, the woman earns as much as he does.

Men and women both contribute to prolonging this custom, perhaps principally from embarrassment: the man does not want to appear to be a gigolo, and the woman does not want to appear to be usurping a male's prerogative. But there are also many men who are unwilling to give up the right of patronage of women, and women either avaricious enough to take advantage or so insecure that they need someone wanting their company enough to pay for it.

Many women envy men the right to take the initiative in intersexual meetings—women spend so much time waiting and hoping for men to make contact. But of course the right to choose and take the initiative is no privilege to a man who lacks the confidence or the skill to make the approach and to risk a refusal. This custom still holds such power that few women will defy it, and comparatively few men are entirely willing to accept such overtures from a woman. Computer dating agencies are well aware of this social order and act on it: the male client gets a list of names to contact; the female client gets none. Like many of the procedures of contact agencies, this makes the system seem like a call-girl service.

Deeply Ingrained

One computer dating agency, with a scrupulously scientific system of questionnaires and computer programing designed by a university cybernetics department, attempted to eliminate this clear injustice. They felt that it was absurd to suppose this Victorian attitude survived in the late twentieth century, particularly with women who were unconventional enough to apply to an agency for partners. They therefore gave women clients lists of names, just as they did men. They found, however, that the old conventions were so deeply ingrained in their women clients that they did not take the initiative. They waited instead for the males to telephone them, as they had been conditioned all their lives to do.

Most computer dating agencies claim that their programing systems are scientifically based, drawn up by psychologists, and uniquely thorough and effective. Many agencies use practically identical questionnaires, however, and many of the questions are either too superficial for the answers to have any real meaning or they are based on fallacious or outdated psychological theories—like questions asking the client's color preferences. Even closely controlled and comprehensive tests of color likes and dislikes are now thought to be not very informative, and a few vague statements on a questionnaire certainly tell nothing about personality.

Usually the client is given two questionnaires: one to fill-in his own particulars, another to list particulars of his ideal partner. With this system, the client has the responsibility for consciously selecting the type of partner he seeks. A few agencies do not allow the client this responsibility. They do not want to know what sort of partner he wants; may select what *they* feel is appropriate for him, according to the philosophy they subscribe to.

Usually questionnaires have the same stock items. There may be some open-ended questions about "yourself" and "your choice," but they are usually put there only to placate the client: it would be very expensive either to feed them into a computer or to register them in hand-sorting systems. Most depend on straightforward multiple-choice sections on personal details (age, height, coloring) and interests (parties, eating out, country walks, poetry, philosophy). Attitudes undergo most scrutiny—attitudes to romantic love and sex, getting on well with other people, having children, pollution, and politics—there may be a direct question about Communism, as civil liberties groups have been disturbed to notice. Clients may also be asked how they feel about receiving

advertising matter in the mail. Such questions disturb people who feel that the agencies may sell their client lists to relevant commercial organizations for sales tactics, as has indeed sometimes occurred. It is usual for agencies to promise full confidentiality regarding all information given to them.

There is little doubt that skillfully designed questionnaires and scrupulous programing *can* succeed in matching people who are attracted to each other and who would tend to continue the friendship beyond one meeting, whether or not it developed into courtship or marriage. Three American psychologists—D. Byrne, C. R. Ervin and J. Lamberth—selected 88 psychology students and paired them off, boy with girl, on the basis of their answers to an attitude and personality questionnaire. Of these, 24 pairs were matched as "highly similar" (they gave the same answers to about two-thirds of the questions asked); the remaining 20 pairs were "less similar" (only a third of their answers coincided).

The pairs were told that this was a computer-determined date and sent off to "get acquainted" for half an hour. Their degree of interpersonal attraction was then noted, first by observing how close they stood to one another, then by written

evaluation—each student rating his partner. The "highly similar" pairs showed a higher level of attraction for each other. Physical attraction influenced the degree of interest, but not enough to contradict the findings. A follow-up made several months later confirmed this finding: "highly similar" pairs were more likely to have dated since the experiment.

The difference between a controlled experiment in the psychology department of a university and the dealings of a commercial organization is that the latter is likely to cut many corners to save money. There are numerous indications that agencies may be matching only one or two characteristics. The only characteristic consistently matched, in fact, is age. Ludicrous mismatches are frequent. Even something as obvious as height may be neglected. A short man will invariably want a small woman, a tall woman a tall man; computer-matching a short man with a tall woman makes for a humiliating meeting for both. Others angered by the system include people who have specified that they are agnostic only to find themselves matched with a Roman Catholic; people who have liberal attitudes matched with strong right-wingers; people who have described themselves as strongly against extramarital sexual intercourse matched with people who are against "marriage as a permanent institution."

One male researcher had a name on his list who was apparently never at home. Every time he rang Sally, her phone was answered by someone who described herself as Sally's flatmate. Every time she said that Sally was out, or ill, or away, or on vacation. He was sure that it was Sally he was speaking to and that she had regretted applying to the agency and was too timid either to accept a date or to tell him that she had decided to drop out.

Because of the way the system works, it is only the female dropout rate that is perceptible; it is impossible to know the numbers of men who do so since no one phones them. Women living in small towns are naturally most prone to change their minds. They fear that the nature of their date may become generally known or that they will actually be acquainted with him already. The anonymity of the big cities makes this less likely.

Since the questionnaire system depends on clients' self-assessment,

John Kingaby

My ideal man is tall and handsome, extremely rich, generous, with a sense of humor and a fast car.

there are also disappointments resulting from dishonesty or self-deceit. The agency never sees the client, so no check is made.

One researcher tested three agencies, getting a total of sixteen names at once. Of these, two were outside the area he had specified; three were not at the address given (one not known; one gone, no address; one returned to her own country a year ago—few agencies keep their books up-to-date). Another was no longer available—she had registered with the agency six months previously, because she and her boyfriend had quarreled; now they were reconciled. Five others, when they met, revealed attitudes directly opposed to those he had asked for. This left five "possibles" out of the original sixteen. None of these five had anything like the occupation he had requested, and none actually fulfilled any of his positive requirements. They were perfectly pleasant, but since the partner he had been promised was described as "one of those few-in-thousands who can communicate with you at a deep level of understanding", he felt that the "matching" process was poor.

Two of his dates told him that they had registered with the agencies because they knew someone who had used them successfully. One knew a 30-year-old divorcée with several children who used it simply to be taken out; one had a flatmate who had become engaged to her computer date.

Just for a Laugh

Comparatively few clients are totally disenchanted with the service offered, although most clients meet each date once only and give up after the first batch. Many try it (or tell themselves that they do so) "just for a laugh", and find it an intriguing experience, if nothing else. The industry is only about ten years old and naturally attracts a lot of attention from all sorts of people. A journalist commissioned to write about dating agencies had registered as an ordinary client with an agency in order to see how the procedure worked. Her first date puzzled her, because he seemed reluctant to talk about himself and unnaturally eager to hear about her. Eventually she discovered that he too was a journalist, posing as an ordinary client in order to write about it. This was one instance of successful matching, at least.

Women may be deprived of the privilege of choosing their computer dates, but they are privileged in another way. A man usually is given

Marshall Cavendish

six names to contact; a woman's name may be put on the lists of many male clients, and she may get a flood of twenty or thirty calls to choose from. The agencies claim many marriages, and certainly marriages do result from these services. One London agency claims an average of 2,000 marriages a year since it started.

Of the various contact organizations, the computer dating system is in fact most likely to benefit someone who is using the service because of social difficulties. Perhaps their poor social skills have repeatedly alienated people they are attracted to, or perhaps they have suffered a broken marriage or a broken engagement and are suddenly alone again. Some may have suffered a long illness—mental or physical. These are all people who need to relearn social skills. The computer system works best for them for two reasons. Firstly, if the questionnaire is any good at all, the client learns a lot about himself in the process of filling it in and also gains self-knowledge in describing his desired partner. Secondly, the computer system supplies more contacts than other more traditional dating bureaus, and having dates with many people in a short time provides a crash course in social learning.

I'll meet you at the station at noon. You'll recognize me because I'll be wearing a red carnation in my lapel.

There is also the possibility that a client underestimates his own abilities, and this is the reason he has found it difficult to relate to people in his customary social contacts. With numbers of new people, there will be a chance of discovering someone who is not only *not* antagonized by his attitudes, but responds to them. Absurdly, the chance of this happening is arguably *greater* with inadequate matching procedures, since they virtually ignore the client's self-assessment in any case. A competent matching system would match him according to his self-assessment, probably landing him with someone equally timid and the relationship would never get off the ground.

Measuring the success of computer dating systems is difficult. For the really inhibited and withdrawn, they probably simply confirm their worst fears about people. But for many they have proven to be a valuable, if temporary, lifeline. And many more have learned a great deal about themselves and others in the process and are able to use improved social skills afterwards to very good effect.

Leaving the nest

As children we depend on our parents for everything, but you can have too much of a good thing—leaning too much can be harmful. Growing up is a matter of finding the right balance.

"No man is an island." John Donne's words go straight to the heart of the human condition. We are a social species, interdependent to a degree which we do not always like to admit.

Beginning with childhood, the human infant is particularly helpless in a complex world, and his dependency on parents and others is prolonged for longer (in proportion to his life span) than any other living creature.

One of the many peculiarities that results from this prolonged dependency—according to psychoanalytic writer Dr. Anthony Storr—is the human tendency towards cruelty. So complete is the child's dependence on others for his every need when very young that his earliest and possibly most enduring notions about the world and his place in it are indelibly printed in his mind by the nature and quality of his interactions with his parents. If he is lucky, he may be thrown into a predominantly loving, rewarding environment; if he is not, he could find himself in a negative, rejecting one which is nearly oblivious to his existence. Because of his dependence there is no escape from it.

Cruelty and Malice

It is thought that the child's affiliative impulses (his feelings of dependency and love for his parents and his desire to be near them), if seriously threatened or rejected, may lead to extreme alarm or defensiveness. This in turn can lead to hateful feelings and cruelty if the rejection persists. One school of thought holds that hate and aggression—and other feelings such as greed, envy and jealousy—are all derivatives of the primary experience of dependency and the conflicts associated with it.

Significantly, in comparison with those of humans, the aggressive acts of animals—possibly because they mature to independence relatively early—are of short duration, without the cruelty and malice which are so often a feature of planned retribution. Bearing grudges and the desire for revenge seem to be uniquely human.

Poets and philosophers have long appreciated that feelings of hate may reside alongside deep feelings of love. Love and hate are opposite sides of the same coin, and this ambivalence indicates the complexity of human emotions. Just as there is a negative side to human dependency relationships there is also the positive aspect of the love and the strength-giving bond that develops between the mem-

David Levin

A clinging child is an insecure child. Dependency is usually the result of the parents' attitude, first scolding but finally giving in.

bers of a happy, close-knit family.

While the rejected child (like the abandoned lover) may respond with hate to his sudden loss the youngster who is nurtured and cherished is fueled for his journey through life by the love he receives in the dependency relationship. It is this love which compels him to give up many of his atavistic impulses, selfish desires and uncharitable inclinations. His wish to please his parents makes him willing to comply with the rules that his parents are teaching him in the name of socialization.

Dr. Karen Horney, the American psychoanalyst, believes that early feelings of helplessness and isolation engender a profound anxiety which gives rise to what might be called dependency strategies. The findings of Dr. Sears and his fellow researchers in child development lend support to this idea. In a study they conducted, 36 percent of the mothers studied were often irritable and punished their children when they clung to them. But it was found that this irritable scolding while pulling themselves away from their clinging children only increased the frequency of such dependency. The most dependent children of all belonged to mothers who, for a time, irritably rejected dependency demands but eventually gave in to them, thus rewarding the child by intermittent reinforcement. This is the most potent type of reinforcer, as it stabilizes patterns of behavior which are being learned.

Comfort Craving

Emotional dependence is a secondary aspect of physical dependence and develops as basic needs are met. After the first few days or weeks an infant will cease crying when picked up before his primary need (usually hunger) is relieved. His mother's mere presence has acquired reward value for him. The goal here is more than mere help: he craves human relationship. Her comforting presence has become a secondary drive in itself.

In most families the child, as he grows up, will tend to obtain a mixture of rewards and punishments for dependent behaviors—and not always in a consistent pattern. He will be required to rely on others in some situations and allowed (or even encouraged) to be autonomous in others. The question of whether a child remains dependent or becomes relatively independent is likely to be contingent upon parental rewards and punishments. Indeed the extent of the child's dependence has been found to

be associated with direct permissiveness for and reinforcement of such behavior.

In Western society, and particularly American society, we lay emphasis on weaning the child away from his absolute dependence on parents and teachers and other adult figures and encourage the development of autonomy. Even without cultural pressures there seems to be an inexorable force propelling the child in the direction of maturity, driving him towards greater independence and self-help. It is a central theme of American child-rearing philosophy that independence training should come early and be fairly comprehensive. The problem is that this can be done too soon. A child needs to be dependent for a year or two, and anything that arouses insecurity over his relationship with his mother may exaggerate his dependency drive instead of decreasing it.

There comes a day when you have to do things for yourself. Even if you make a mess it doesn't matter, because you're learning slowly but surely what growing up is about.

The mother who is considerate of her child's needs and gentle in helping him to move from one phase to another is more likely to see him grow up to be independent.

In working out guidelines to facilitate a child's mastery of the environment, parents need to remember that a child passes through stages in which he demands different kinds of support from his parents. At the earliest stage this support is essentially physical and involves the satisfaction of his basic needs, especially for physical contact, food and warmth, and environmental stability. Next the child requires support in his exploration of the physical and social world he lives in, as he handles objects and plays various roles. Finally, the child seeks support in his attempt to follow rules and conform to norms. At every stage the child demands parental support in both the recognition and confirmation of himself as a certain kind of being.

First he needs to be recognized as a *dependent* individual in need of nurture, contact and comfort. Later on, he wishes to be recognized as a *doer*. He desires to be seen and to have his real or imagined achievements appreciated by others—an audience. Finally, he wants to be confirmed as a *good* creature who plays the game of life correctly and decently.

Healthy personality development and satisfactory social relationships can be described in terms of finding a balance between the child's need to make demands on others and his ability to recognize the demands which others make on him: there must be a sort of equilibrium between dependence and independence. At certain stages of life there are crises when this balance becomes disturbed: conflict crises over the incompatible demands between parent and child, over obeying the rules or doing your own thing, and over clinging metaphorically to a state of dependency and being independent and grownup.

Sense of Inadequacy

From feelings of omnipotence brought about because the infant gets his own way, the child comes to realize his relative impotence given his state of total helplessness in the wider scale of things. Gradually, the child has to adapt to his parents' will as he gets older and more capable of doing things for himself. Some theorists believe that the infant's sense of adequacy or self-esteem depends upon his misinterpretation of his parents' earliest subservience to his will and needs, as a result of which he exaggerates his volitional power and autonomy. He is in for a letdown as he gets older and has to moderate his demands—except in the case of those mothers who do not allow their children to be emotionally weaned from them. Parents differ in the timing and the degree to which they encourage a baby's transition from a totally "demanding" to a partly "demand-obeying" status. Many individuals never develop a strong commitment to the more abstract forms of reciprocity.

At adolescence there can be another crisis because of the ambiguity of the demands adults make on the teenager to be grown-up and independent while not giving them the

freedom and responsibility.

Although Felicity was only 16, she had to carry many adult responsibilities. Because her mother and father both worked she spent much of her time mothering her two younger brothers. She would see that they had something to eat and drink when they came home from school, would tend to their cuts and bruises, and hear their confidences when they were low in spirits or disturbed by a harsh teacher or a bully at school. She did most of the shopping for the family and would plan a week ahead what would be required for family meals. She also played a major part in seeing to housework and the laundry. Felicity was happy to do these things as she considered herself a member of a loving and warm family.

Double Standards

But her parents refused to give her the same measure of responsibility when it came to her personal freedom. They were very wary about her going to camp with a mixed group of boys and girls of her age. She told them that their refusals to let her go away on vacation with friends demeaned her by implying that she was not to be trusted sexually. They denied this inference hotly but then again would seem to confirm it by being particularly strict about the boys she went out with and by waiting up to see what time she came in. They told her it was their love and concern for her which caused them to be what she termed overprotective, not distrust. She said that on the one hand she was treated as a child and on the other given duties (which she accepted happily) that were those of an adult: they could not have it both ways.

In our culture adolescence can be a very trying time because of this ambiguity about the young person's role in society. He may have to fight for his country and die for it at an age when he cannot vote. He is appealed to by advertisers as an adult with money to spend on their products and yet he is patronized as being unable to arrive at considered and well-judged conclusions about his own actions. Part of the problem is that we pay lip service to the ideal of producing what is known as the altruistic-autonomous character. We say in our society that we want our children to grow up into the sort of people whose morality is internalized and based upon the desire to live up to positive values rather than simply the craven fear of breaking rules.

A person of this kind chooses the

rules he lives by and feels free to modify them with experience. Abandoning all moral controls is a real option for the autonomous character, but he is unlikely to take it up because, of all the different character types, he is most aware of the roots of morality in personal relationships and therefore most likely to find morality self-evident. He is usually successful in resisting temptation, but when he does transgress his code he deals with his shortcomings in a constructive manner. He is altruistic and generous; his moral reasoning is based upon general principles which are rational and applied flexibly and with originality. His moral ideology is constantly developing.

Research into child-rearing techniques suggests that this sort of character is produced by a happy home in which democratic interactions with adults are frequent and where attachments to adults and to the peer group are nicely balanced, so that the child is stimulated to grow up somewhere between them—neither identified with the one nor the other.

There must also be a balance between the overly indulgent (permissive) and overly restrictive and dominating (authoritarian) approaches to child rearing and discipline. The children of domineering mothers usually lack self-reliance and ability to cope realistically with their problems and later on fail or are slow to accept adult responsibilities. They are apt to be submissive and overly obedient and withdraw from situations they find difficult to deal with.

Feared and Revered

Many of us reach adulthood without resolving our childhood needs to be dependent on mother figures and father figures. Frank was brought up in a home ruled by a stern and somewhat distant Victorian father. He both feared and revered this man and, sadly, could never quite live up to his strict and high standards. Frank's mother was a rather submissive, long-suffering woman. Like her husband she was very religious, belonging to a particularly strict and puritanical Christian sect. Her own life was ringed round with morally restrictive rules and she put the same straightjacket of suffocating restrictions on the life of her growing child.

Over the years this combination turned Frank into what is called an authoritarian character. He had a great need to look uncritically and deferentially to those with status and power. He believed that rules were there to be obeyed and that the trouble with the American way of life was that it was not tough enough. He believed that democracy led to weakness and a loss of moral fiber. Indeed he felt a dictatorship which insisted on the authority of the law by means of much harsher sanctions would soon bring America to its rightful place in the world—looked up to and respected by the other nations (especially some of the upstart countries that continually criticized the United States). He felt very strongly that various minority groups in America were paid too much heed and that the young—whose indiscipline he deprecated—were dignified with a far too important role and too much say in society. Here then, in Frank, we see one kind of dependency in adult life; such a person has a need to depend on strong, dictatorial father-figures and a too ready willingness to defer to those in authority.

The Happy Martyr

At a more personal level, there are the unresolved dependencies which men and women take over from their childhood attitudes and relationships with their parents into their marriages and friendships in adult life. Dennis had been grossly overprotected by his mother from early childhood. He had developed severe asthma at the age of three, and on many nights his father would be displaced from the conjugal bed so that Dennis could lie with his mother and be tended to during his severe bouts of suffocating asthma.

Not unnaturally his mother became particularly attentive to the slightest signs of ill health in her child; she would dress him too warmly and be too insistent that he come in early from his play so as not to get damp. She tended to overmedicate him and to be on the watch all the time that he did not come to any harm.

This pampering turned Dennis into a rather timid child, afraid to take risks and to try out things for himself. He preferred the protective company of his mother to the fellowship of his peers. When the time came for him to go to school, he went through severe bouts of anxiety and a period of refusing to attend. Special exemptions were arranged so that he could get out of physical education and sports. In many ways he was made to feel that he was the center of his mother's universe and that she orbited around him, the sole purpose of her existence being to see to his needs.

The mother happily martyred herself to this role in life and during the years

Marshall Cavendish

that he grew up she enjoyed telling her friends how many lost nights of sleep there had been, of how many tribulations she suffered as she took him from specialist to specialist looking for a cure, and how her overwhelming concern for his delicate health had, in the end, strained her relationship with her husband. Before he left her her husband said, "Why don't you marry the poor child and get it done with?"

Submissive Sympathy

After many trials and tribulations with girlfriends not approved by his mother, Dennis at the age of 30 at last got married. To his intense surprise his wife was reluctant to take on a maternal role or to devote her life to waiting on and nursing (as she put it when overwhelmed by frustration) a "sickly man-child." When she stood up to his more outrageous demands for dependency, he would regress and have childlike tantrums. These would be followed by severe paroxysms of breathing difficulty which she suspected to be psychosomatic. More often than not, when these failed to win her submissive sympathy, he would make for home and the ready ministrations of his mother. Not surprisingly, given an unwillingness on

This is when it all starts. A baby is born frail and helpless and so is dependent on its mother for everything. It is she who protects and provides it with a constant supply of food, warmth and love.

the part of both partners to give in, this marriage broke down and Dennis returned to a bachelor's life with his mother. His wife decided that if she were to marry again she'd choose a man who had long ago left his mother.

In far less pathological situations, we all try to resolve our minor conflicts between our needs to be dependent on others (as we were in childhood) and our needs to be autonomous and mature, self-determined people. When we have children we are impelled, by the new obligations and duties we assume, to be grown-up and independent. Tragedies do occur when immature and still-dependent people have children and cannot adjust to the independent, caring role that has been thrust upon them. In the end, of course, we are all dependent on one another to some extent. Family life provides a context in which we can all give and take the nurturance and succor that we crave. Everyone needs to pamper and be pampered.

Head Office

Men of rank

Butter wouldn't melt in his mouth before the election, but once a politician's home and dry it's a different story. When corruption sets in, success doesn't smell so sweet.

"I have come to the conclusion," General de Gaulle is said to have once observed, "that politics is too serious a matter to be left to politicians." Speaking as perhaps the last of the great European statesmen—as opposed to mere politicians—he did not, unfortunately, go on to declare whom politics should be left to.

History has shown that the only real alternative to an elected government or one-party system is military rule, and for the armed forces of any country to involve themselves in politics is a sure recipe for disaster—as Greece and Portugal have discovered.

However, there can be little doubt that de Gaulle had himself in mind as an alternative to the politicians, if by "politics" he meant "running the affairs of the country." Interpreted in that way, the remark rises above the level of an after-dinner epigram and begins to make some sort of sense, for, unlike totalitarian regimes, democracies face a fundamental problem when it comes to managing the country's social and economic affairs.

Those who are elected to do the job—to create the policies, make the decisions, and superintend their execution—are extremely unlikely to

be the ones best equipped with the right skills for the task.

The constant threat to the very foundations of democracy is that the wrong men are voted into power for the wrong reasons. It is only the stabilizing and conservative influence of the armed forces, the judiciary, and the civil service which keeps politicians in line. When these fail, democracy breaks down. Nazi Germany produced the most extreme example of this collapse.

Theoretically, in democracies, the will of more than half the people is supposed to be expressed in the politi-

cal process, through the election of candidates who have espoused this or that policy, leaving aside the question of whether the man in the street with his relative lack of information is the best one to decide how the country should be run. If the democratic system worked as its idealists wished, candidates would step forward at election time as champions of various causes and with policies to suit.

If they were elected, this would indicate that their policies had the support of most people in their constituencies. If they were not elected, they would gracefully withdraw from the contest. Unfortunately, democratic politics have now become professionalized to the extent that policies take second place to the need to be elected, which produces a number of highly undesirable consequences. The most obvious of these is that since candidates and the parties they represent will invent policies designed primarily to secure

the maximum number of votes, these policies will actually often be detrimental to the country as a whole.

The commonest trap is to offer bribes to the electorate in the form of increased welfare facilities or tax concessions which the national coffers are later unable to pay for. Election pledges are then either met, at the expense of national bankruptcy, or not met, in which case the elected members have to engage in political maneuvering to cover up their broken promises. This, in turn, results in a gradual loss of credibility for the politicians in question. The electorate turns cynical, loses confidence in its representatives and finally becomes indifferent to the entire system. And that opens the door to still further abuses.

At the same time, since it is a commonplace to accuse politicians of duplicity and hypocrisy, if not outright corruption, and since there are no apparent remedies for it, it is all too

easy to lose sight of the need for nonstop vigilance over the political system. Unfortunately, public complacency about the moral fiber, or lack of it, of politicians leads only to more and more abuse of the system. Equally unfortunately, while this sort of complacency exists, the public is content merely to demand, "What does it matter if politicians are all sanctimonious hypocrites and double-dealers, providing they run the country properly?" And attitudes like this present two key problems of their own. In the first place, when people talk about "running the country properly," they usually mean "running it to *my* relative advantage." Secondly—and this is perhaps the most damning indictment of public complacency—such attitudes actually encourage politicians to develop the wrong set of skills—skills that help them to get elected and then to stay in office once they have been elected. And these

David Godfrey

The makings of a puppet government. Big money can be useful for pulling strings behind the scenes.

skills are not the skills needed to manage a society or an economy.

As Professor Rapaport points out in his *Conflict in the Man-Made Environment,* "The professionalism of politics, particularly in the United States, has paralleled the professionalization of competitive business. The *product,* whether that of politics (supposedly 'policies') or that of business (supposedly goods and services), becomes of secondary importance, relevant only to the extent that it contributes to the success of the professionals, whether businessmen or politicians. The primary skills in these professions are directed towards activities relevant to the making of careers, contributing to increasing profits or expanding business, or to successfully mobilizing votes."

It is virtually impossible to reconcile this situation with professed altruistic motives. To talk about "a career in politics" automatically implies self-advancement. At the same time, since the essential skill of politicians is in getting elected, candidates are rarely required to put themselves on the line as individuals; indeed they tend to avoid it unless it will gain votes. Consequently it is almost impossible to determine the individual's motives for seeking election behind the electioneering smokescreen until it is too late. Anyone who has managed to become adopted by a major party has probably already succeeded in disguising his true feelings, opinions and ambitions from the selection committee. He has come that far by telling people what they want to hear. It is only once the candidate is in office that his real motives will emerge.

Few people would disagree with Lord Acton's observation "Power tends to corrupt and absolute power corrupts absolutely. Great men are almost always bad men." And while it is true to say that no one enters politics at all seriously unless he is seeking power, politicians' motives for seeking power differ greatly according to the political system and its cultural background, not to mention financial and social circumstances.

Under a totalitarian regime, Communist or Fascist, both political and economic power is vested in the Party bureaucracy. To take the Soviet Union as an example, the only way of achieving elite status is through the Party machine. So the ambitious comrade has to become a good Party member if he wants to get anywhere at all. Even if he has risen through the ranks outside the Party to join the intelligentsia and has thereby won a certain degree of enhanced material comfort and social status, he has no say in events beyond his own sphere—no voice, no control, and no real authority.

It is only to be expected that since the Party bureaucracy provides the sole route to wielding authority it attracts a high proportion of people with authoritarian personalities. There is no other way for them to express themselves. Even though the legendary tyranny of petty Party functionaries under Stalin's rule has long since been whittled down and a measure of autonomy granted to industrial managers and other professions, the

Party monolith remains unshakable, its ideology intact. Since there is no provision for dissent within the political system, no one enters politics from any progressive, reforming motive.

While in the Soviet Union, along with all other dictatorships, professional political success depends exclusively on persuading those above you in the Party hierarchy of your ideological zeal without reference to the public at large, the situation in the United States is almost exactly the reverse. There, popular acclaim is the only route to political success, from the lowest ranks of municipal politics right up to president. No one in actual political office is ever appointed, except in unusual circumstances.

However, the American democratic beliefs, being sanctified by and enshrined in the Constitution, form an ideology as immutable as the Soviets'. There is no provision in the American system for changing the fundamental tenets of democracy as the Americans have interpreted it. Such a high degree of institutional stability, comparable with that of the Russian system, provides the basis for an equiva-

lent degree of professionalism.

Since high office—municipal, state or national—can be achieved only by winning popular acclaim and converting this to votes, and since the campaign needed to mobilize such popularity costs vast sums of money, only the very rich, or those with heavy financial backing, need apply. Since, also, no one becomes rich (with the possible exception of film stars) or acquires financial support by embracing dubious radical politics, the American system, like the Russian, secures its continued survival by ensuring that only devotees of the status quo are allowed to compete in the race.

Only Lip Service

Theoretically, a free economy should be able to take care of itself with minimal interference from politicians. And, providing industry develops a social conscience more or less in tune with influential pressure groups, the system survives. Unfortunately, the very fact that surviving along with it is an alarming incidence of extreme poverty and racial intolerance suggests that new politicians are sufficiently interested in social reform

Although political conventions seem brimful of spontaneous enthusiasm, the boys in the back room often know the final count long before the first ballot's been cast.

to pay it more than lip service.

Ironically, it is in Western-type democracies' noblest aspirations that their greatest weakness lies. Freedom of speech, freedom of political allegiance, and freedom of industrial action allow the most bizarre and dangerous people to rise to power by ostensibly legitimate means. At the same time, the very absence of conformity, which is the hallmark of an ideal democracy, makes it far more difficult for the party in power to run the country's affairs when times are hard and when what is needed is cooperation and control rather than individual initiative. The temptation for leaders to seize complete power out of a sense of frustration at their inability to balance the nation's books, which they blame on people's refusal to cooperate voluntarily, is not difficult to understand.

It is even more ironic that Britain, who taught democracy to half the world, should be the most prominent

victim of democracy's Achilles heel: Britain has sacrificed solvency for freedom. There might be a sort of pathetic nobility in this state of affairs had it been the result of a last-ditch decision by a group of high-minded men of principle. The fact, however, is that, though solvency has indeed been sacrificed, so has freedom, and both sacrifices were made on the altar of dogma while the nation's leaders stood by, victims of their own duplicity.

British politicians, once described as "animals who can sit on a fence and keep both ears to the ground," are a motley group representing all shades of opinion, a great array of interest groups and covering the entire political spectrum in a way that is impossible within either the Soviet Union or the United States. However, the wide differences in political belief do not disguise the fact that European politicians fall into four distinct caricatures (however harsh) when it comes to analyzing their individual motives, often irrespective of political color.

First, the *extremists,* of left or right, are misguided utopians and disenchanted idealists who may have set out with the noblest of intentions, whose ideals have ossified into dogma which they now use as a substitute for creative thought. They are often authoritarian personalities of bureaucratic union background, whose ambitions have outstripped their abilities and who are consequently bitter, resentful and humorless. They are identifiable by their intransigence, intolerance, automatic behavior and symptoms of paranoia.

The *reformers,* again of left or right, are those who have entered politics out of a genuine desire to work for the greater good. Often mocked as liberal do-gooders, a handful manage to remain political virgins with their honor intact. They avoid making extravagant promises and remain champions of worthy causes. They crusade against injustice without achieving high office. Those whose political honor survives are destined, by definition, for political backwaters. The rest are bound to defect to other groups if they want to make their presence felt, usually abandoning their earlier declared missions while pretending not to.

Playing the Game

The *dilettantes* are a group comprising millionaire socialists, practicing lawyers, company directors, and others with large private incomes. It is this group C. Northcote Parkinson must have had in mind when he wrote, in *Parkinson's Law,* "The British, being brought up on team games, enter their House of Commons in the spirit of those who would rather be doing something else. If they cannot be playing golf or tennis, they can at least pretend that politics is a game with very similar rules."

The *professionals* form the most effective and potentially the most dangerous group, since it is composed of career politicians who must, by definition, be motivated to a substantial extent by self-interest. At its best, this group provides strong, unequivocal and relatively honest leadership. At worst, its actions are based solely on political expediency. Regrettably, these are the professionals who tend to achieve high office, cheerfully exaggerating at the polls,

A show of hands for the Liberal candidate. Before the libel laws were tightened, politicians were often publicly accused of corruption.

delighting in political maneuvers and manipulations, and engaging in vulgar grubbing for personal advantage.

In this group there are a number of defectors from the extremist group who are perhaps the most dangerous of all, since they are likely to be obsessional neurotics who combine duplicity with fanaticism. At the same time, it is among the professionals that delusions of grandeur are most effectively nurtured. The chief problem is that not only do professional politicians change their allegiances with their shirts, but they convince themselves that political sleight of hand is the same thing as government.

Clearly, unless anarchy is to prevail, someone or some group has to run a country's social and economic affairs. Somebody has to peacefully resolve conflicts between various interest groups. It should not be too much to ask of a civilized society that its leaders be honest and honorable men. The responsibility for the fact that they are not must rest with the public who, in its indifference, elected them.

It is all very well and indeed understandable for people to become bemused by the posturing and utterances of politicians, for, as Adlai Stevenson said, "A politician is a statesman who approaches every question with his mouth open." But public indifference encourages political abuse, and political abuse leads to corruption, demagoguery, and the erosion of liberty. Unfortunately, voters get the politicians they deserve.

Kim Saver

End of the affair

The song is over, but the melody lingers on—and you can't get her face out of your mind.

It would be easier, thought Peter, if there were lawyers to conduct an affair. They would make it so much more clear-cut. Instead, it was a messy business, a zone of uncertainties from beginning to end.

Until his three-year affair with Martha broke up, that very uncertainty had been one of its chief attractions; now it meant that he was not sure whether the affair had ended or not.

Peter had known a married couple to conduct their own divorce, have a celebration lunch afterwards and then live together for a week. That was enough to reassure them they had made the right decision. From then on they knew it was safer to be friends.

Peter had been conducting his own "divorces" long before Martha, each with peculiar lack of success. It was paradoxical, he thought, that those who were married foolishly sought to take matters into their own hands while he, who had always been free to do so, longed for the law's support.

It was a universal trend that marriages were becoming more amateurish while affairs were becoming increasingly professional. The law was backing away from the one and bolstering the other. Peter believed it was high time someone else sorted out his affairs.

Some men, he knew, were strong enough—or was it lucky enough—to walk out of an affair cleanly, without a trace of it remaining on them. Some women could neatly excise from their

Marshall Cavendish

affections a score of men or more without flinching between embraces. Others were able, like the divorced couple that Peter had known, to drift pleasantly into fresh fields of friendship that enabled them to introduce each other to their subsequent lovers. Peter could do neither. He had presumed, when you part, you parted for good. He had found, to his distress, that the finality of that act was open to widely differing interpretations.

What led up to his affair with Martha, how that affair was conducted, and what caused its immediate breakdown are all part of another story. When Peter found himself alone at last in the apartment they had so violently shared, he was at once confronted by a parade of problems. Some of these were practical, others were emotional. All of them concerned Martha in one way or another. She might as well not have left.

Peter considered the practical problems. In the first week of the breakup, he saw Martha twice. By careful arrangement in more halcyon days they worked in the same area of town, in the same street, within a few doors. They visited the same bars; they liked walking in the same parks; they both had the same doctor; since they had split the "custody" of their two cats between them, they also shared a vet. And as Martha's sister, with whom she had temporarily gone to stay, lived only a couple of blocks away, they used the same transport and shopped in the same stores. It was fortunate, thought Peter, that they did not also work in the same office: the whole thing would have become impossible.

Introspective Moping

As it was, it was incumbent on Peter to change his way of life, since it was he who had thrown Martha out, not she who had left him. There were certain rules, even in this unstructured game. So he left for work at an ungodly hour and returned far later than he liked to. He shopped in his lunch hour. He changed his doctor and his vet.

After he passed Martha once in the street at lunchtime, he had sandwiches brought to his office, thus depriving himself of one of his chief pleasures of the day at the local restaurants. Another time, he went for a long, soulful walk in his favorite park and to his fury saw in the distance Martha and her sister walking also.

No one wants to hear that love is dead, but sometimes it has to be said.

Peter then discovered that he might be forced to change his friends as well, if he really meant to avoid Martha. After a few days of self-indulgence, expanding his personality in the new freedom of his empty apartment (others might call it a period of introspective moping), he decided it was time to make the round of his friends—a new man, open to new introductions. He found that Martha had been there first.

The treacherous couple to whose house she had invited herself for dinner had been their best friends. Peter fondly imagined they had merely tolerated Martha, who had often antagonized them openly. When he challenged them for what he termed their "deceitful" hospitality, they remarked that they really quite enjoyed Martha and anyway she had called them and how could they refuse? Indignant at being deprived of a good dinner in good company simply because Martha had got there first, Peter reappraised his relationship with his friends. Clearly, he could no longer safely drop in on them without notice.

Peter had often imagined all the people he would get in touch with when he was free—people he wanted to see alone, women he wanted to know better, without the censorious eye of Martha. He saw them. They had seen Martha. Martha, so his friends told him, had seen him with them. Life was less private than ever. Was it coincidence or Martha's contrivance?

Instead of forgetting Martha, Peter found himself intrigued to know how she knew so much. Instead of being relieved to be rid of her recently infuriating presence, he found himself curious as to why so many mutual friends continued to be in touch with her. What did they suddenly see in her? Was he missing out on something? It was no good when they said, What else could we do—she keeps on calling us and demanding to know if we've seen you; he did not wholly believe them. He had thought they would have been as relieved as he that they had separated. That was his ego. Now he wondered what he had lost.

A Curt Note

If he thought that the affair itself had been conducted along tactical and strategical lines of perverse genius, Peter was now aware that this period of realignment was to employ far more devious maneuvers, as well as tricks of the utmost simplicity. By the time eleven people had phoned within the first week to ask either for Martha's new number or for some small piece of information that they knew Peter would know because Martha knew it too, Peter was convinced that Martha had put them up to it.

In the second week, he had five phone calls from friends of Martha (How did she acquire new friends so quickly?) of whom he had never heard who explained that Martha had left some object or other in the apartment and could they come and collect it for her. Peter concluded that she had carefully hidden these objects around the apartment for just such future negotiation. He made a thorough search and sent all the remaining things to her sister. A few days later he received a curt note from Martha herself, reminding him that *if* he was thinking of having a clearance sale, there *were* a couple of record albums that were *hers*, that he had given to her. She would like them. A similar exchange took place a week later over the subject of some books. Peter knew he was beaten.

His first collapse of determination occurred when Martha actually phoned him to ask without preamble whether or not he intended to go with her to the zoo, since this was the time of year when they habitually went. When he attempted to demur, she burst out with, "For God's sake, it's not as if we've had a divorce"—to which there was little reply. He was curious to see what she was like; more basically and selfishly, he wanted to reassure himself that even if she had already started an affair with someone else he was still able to draw her back, just in case he did decide he could cope with her.

Second Round

They went. It was very pleasant. They stayed the night together. The next day, she said that she had arranged to go out of town and see his parents. *His* parents. They had called them her out-laws. Of course he would come, she asked. He felt trapped completely. They quarreled bitterly over whether or not her visit was a presumption, and she left for the country alone, furious. A very nice day, said his parents later; quite a surprise, she really was on her best behavior, we did enjoy seeing her, what a pity you can't make it up—after all, it's not as if you've had a divorce or anything . . . a lover's tiff, that's all.

He had presumed, as his divorced acquaintances assured him with smug satisfaction, that a single man of his age—on the knife-edge of thirty —would be much in demand. He looked forward to the invitations with pleasure. He would avoid affairs in the future; it would be accepted that only dalliance could be expected from a man so recently set free. So his acquaintances assured him.

Reality was rather different. What kudos there were to be gained from being single and separated belonged only, it seemed, to the divorced. It was only the man who escaped his boring marriage or the "Mrs." who reverted to "Ms." who became objects of curiosity in the social circuit; the man who had recovered from an affair was merely back to square one. Still single at thirty? . . . eyebrows were raised. Instead of dalliance, any woman about whom he maneuvered envisaged another solid affair with marriage a forethought. The teasing pleasures that the divorcé enjoyed became for Peter formidable entanglements. Those light liaisons to which he had looked forward were loaded suddenly with the heavy platitudes of implicit and impending permanence.

Permanence was what Martha had in mind. So did Peter, only his mind dwelt on permanent separation. What a pity you had an affair, said Martha's mother; you might have got married. It was just this lack of definition in their relationship that had caused the tensions between them; and it was the

When a love affair runs down, you may find you have time on your hands.

lack of definition in their separation that caused equal tensions to Peter in the aftermath. Once again, he wished for lawyers.

He considered the emotional problems. They, too, were compounded by a lack of definition. Divorces had their fair share of emotional upset but also had certain advantages. Divorce did not usually take place until both sides were absolutely sure they could no longer tolerate the situation—or until the intolerance of one side overcame the tolerance of the other. An affair might end at a much earlier stage in the deterioration of the relationship—after all, what was the point in trying beyond a certain stage? Even in this so-called enlightened age, there was not the same degree of commitment in an affair. It was supposedly simpler to give up. In spite of this, however, Peter found that he had a great many more sensitive nerve ends than he had counted on.

Tears and Torrents

There was—he did not wish to overdramatize but nonetheless at first there was—the sensation that Martha was dead. He half-believed this, half-imposed it on himself to make sure he would accept that he must do without her (he could not deny that he had been fond of her and would miss her). This sensation was quickly overcome when she phoned two nights after leaving him. She spoke in tears, in torrents, with profuse apologies and promises of anything he wanted, with scarcely hidden threats of suicide which he knew she would not carry through. He was firm in his refusal. But clearly she was not dead, as his friends and his own sightings of her reminded him.

She continued to exist. Without him. Perhaps *he* was dead? To reassure himself that this was not so, he plunged beneath the sheets whenever possible with whomever he could —until he discovered that their intent was less frivolous than his own. In the process he learned several things about himself and Martha.

For a start, the initial allure of a new bedmate, made delicious by the freshness of a new style and the mutual tolerance of combined curiosity, quickly wore off. To give any one of them any kind of substance required an exhausting period of building up mutual experiences. In the rejuvenation therapy that Peter had prescribed for himself, there was no time for that: he must move on—chiefly this meant he must move away from the dangers of involvement. But he sadly missed the delights of shared memories.

Such memories had been the foundation of his affair with Martha. They were ineradicable. Like Martha, they sprang up everywhere, reminding him of things they had shared. It takes a long time, thought Peter, to build up a repertoire like that; it becomes a valuable asset. A fresh eye on new experiences may be a welcome relief but after a time it can become an effort to start again and again. In any case, there was no denying those experiences they had had together. Peter had looked forward to someone new beside him; now there were too many times when he thought that he wished it was Martha, who he knew would like what he liked and appreciate something particular that he enjoyed.

This led him, naturally, to compare his subsequent liaisons to his affair with Martha. This was unrealistic. Nothing could compare with Martha, he reminded himself: nothing could compare with her sandpaper technique of irritation, her forestlike silences, forbidding as the densely packed trees, her pervasive anger and her glum frowns.

But Peter knew that was not what he meant. He was certainly relieved to be rid of that, but he missed her vivacity and energy, the acuteness of her observation, her illogicality. On the other hand, he did not miss it, because she now timed her communications with him on whatever trivial matter with brilliant precision just when he imagined he was beginning to consign her to the past.

Vague Hope

Peter had always wanted a period in their relationship when he could stand back from it and see what it looked like, take stock, reassess. With both of them on top of each other in the apartment, it had been impossible —and yet to talk of a "trial" separation, as certain marriages attempted, was absurd. They never worked; they never resettled.

Parting was the only solution, the only way to get far enough back. And yet he did so with the vague hope that he would want her again. That, Peter knew, was his failing: he wanted her on his own terms. That was one of the differences between marriage and an affair. Some marriages collapsed because one partner or the other was determined to stick to his own terms but, by definition almost, the longer any affair continued the more it existed on one person's terms.

Both partners lived in hope: one of marriage, the other of some other solution. All the cards were with the other partner, in whose hands it was to opt for marriage in the end, to continue the affair as long as he or she could, or to bring it to a close. What Peter had resented, in his particular case, was that the onus was always on him. Martha watched, waited and sulked: not an encouraging incentive to such a notable decision as marriage, remembered Peter.

What his friends pointed out to him—those faithless friends—made him even more stubborn. It seemed to them, they said, that the situation had hardly changed. It was in Peter's hands still to make the decision. Martha, whatever she did, was still waiting. How long did he want to stand back? If he waited until *he* was ready, she might not be there. It was not, they repeated, as if the two of them had had a divorce. Why didn't they get on with their life together and save everyone else a lot of trouble?

Merry-go-round

There was in the end, Peter discovered, only one independent solution. It turned out to be not so independent as he had hoped. He threw himself into another affair—full-blooded and with his eyes open, the thing he had said he would never do again. It was the only way to replace Martha. He knew, anyway, that she had taken another steady lover.

The affair lasted several months with great success. Peter enjoyed the contrast with Martha immensely. He treated the girl with consideration and, instead of being appalled as he might have expected, was surprised to find that he was pleased that she became as possessive as Martha had been. But when she wanted to marry, their positions at the opposite poles of this argument became entrenched. The situation had not changed. The solution depended on Peter. He made the same decision and confronted the same problems, though to a limited degree in view of the shorter period of their affair. And to those problems there was only one solution—another affair . . . and so on round the merry-go-round.

When Peter considered the matter in the irrational light of his own feelings, it was clear to him that he would have done better to have stuck with Martha—not easier but more fun than this endless orbit. To forget his second subsequent affair, he tried to turn back to her, but restarting an old affair had problems of its own that Peter barely dreamed of. There was no telling where it would all end.

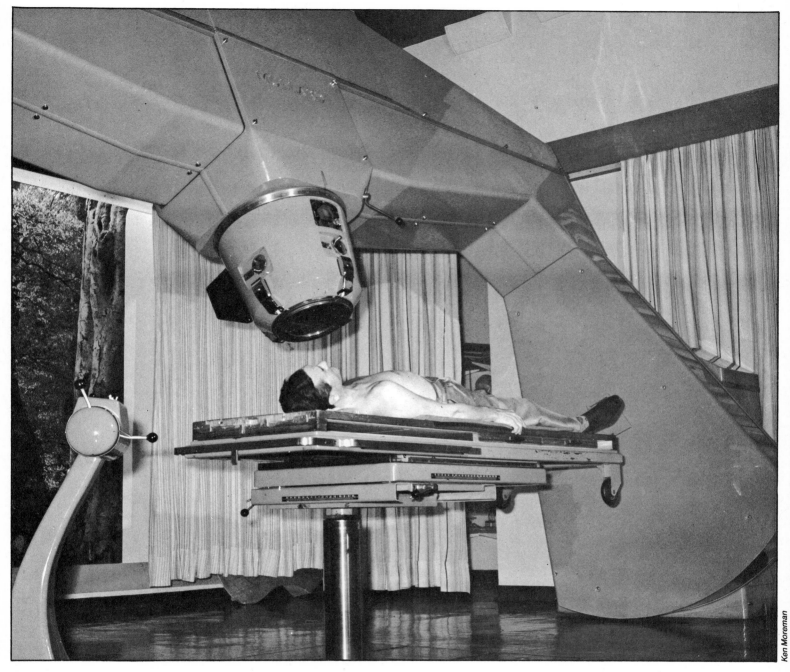

Ken Moreman

Malignant growth

The forbidden word—some horoscopes even refer to those born under Cancer as Moon Children.

In any language in the world, mention of the word "cancer" is something of a social taboo. When a member of the family is known to have cancer, relatives will seldom discuss the illness openly, as if actually to name the disease would ensure the death of the sufferer. Once cancer is diagnosed, the rest of the family begin to behave as if the sufferer is already dead, and most people still think of the disease as being almost invariably fatal. In fact it is not; cancer kills less than half its

victims, in contrast to the almost 100 percent mortality with rabies, from which only one person has ever recovered. So why should cancer be such a terrifying illness? Why cannot it be discussed openly? How does it arise in the first place?

The most disturbing feature of cancer is that it is not a disease in the sense of illness caused by invading germs or by the inevitable aging of the body. Cancer is a relatively minor malfunction of a normal body process

Bombarding deep-seated tumors with X-radiation is just one method of combating the dread disease.

—the replacement of cells. But this minor malfunction can eventually lead to disruption of the major organs of the body and then to death or protracted illness.

All the cells in the body, except for nerve cells, regularly die off and are replaced by the division of adjacent cells. In the human embryo, all the

2791

cells are dividing rapidly, causing development to progress from the single fertilized egg cell into a miniature human being at birth. If, during this period of rapid cell division, part of an organ is removed or damaged, other cells can proliferate to replace the damaged part. This process continues into adulthood in organs like the liver, which can regenerate itself after extensive damage. However, both in a self-repairing organ like the liver and in the entire body as it nears maturity, the dividing cells seem to "know" when to stop. The human animal does not continue to grow indefinitely.

Cancer cells, however, seem to have lost the ability to switch off at the correct time, continuing to multiply at the expense of the surrounding tissue. This can even be demonstrated in a simple glass dish in the laboratory. When normal human cells are cultured in a dish they spread out across the glass in a layer one cell deep. When they reach the edge of the dish, cell division eases, leaving just a thin sheet of cells. But when cancer cells are cultured, they multiply in tangled heaps and form a thickened nodule. When this happens inside the body, a tumor or solid cancer results.

The cells making up the tumor are nourished by the blood, and so they can continue to multiply indefinitely. As the tumor swells, it takes over the surrounding tissue and destroys its functions. If it develops in a gland, the secretions of the gland will eventually cease as the tumor grows. It may involve the walls of a blood vessel. The cells making up the walls of an artery are specially adapted to withstand the pressure of blood, but the cells of a tumor are undifferentiated and have no mechanical strength. The wall may rupture, and a hemorrhage result.

Variety of Symptoms

A tumor developing in the brain will press on the delicate neural tissue and by pressure alone can cause a variety of defects ranging from dizziness and headaches to paralysis and death. If it develops in the long bones of the limbs, a tumor can weaken the structure and fractures may result. Tumors can develop in any organ or part of the body but most commonly appear in just a few areas.

Once a tumor has begun to grow, there is a possibility of individual cells or clumps of cells breaking off and being carried away in the bloodstream. These cancer cells may lodge elsewhere in the body and continue to develop, producing secondary tumors

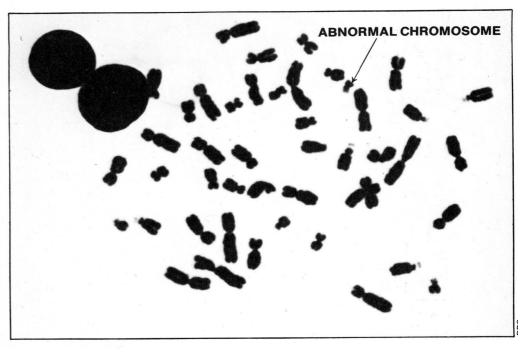

ABNORMAL CHROMOSOME

called metastases. They may also be carried in the lymphatic system, which drains fluid from the body cavities and returns it to the bloodstream. Secondary tumors may develop in the lymph nodes, small structures which filter out bacteria and other material but may allow cancer cells to lodge and develop. Once secondary tumors have developed, the disease can become generalized throughout the body, and at this late stage it may possibly be very difficult to treat.

Secondary Tumors

In practice, secondary tumors often appear in a predictable manner. In breast cancer, secondary tumors may appear in the lymph nodes in the armpits or in the vertebrae of the spine. Lung cancer often causes secondary tumors in the brain, and cancer of the rectum may be followed by liver cancer. Obviously, if the disease can be recognized early enough, while there is only one tumor, there is a better chance of treatment.

This sequence of events is by no means inevitable. Although cancer cells are derived from our own tissues, and so not immediately destroyed as invaders by the body's immunity system, they are different enough to produce some immune response. But the substances produced by the body as a defense against cancer can seldom kill all the proliferating cells. Instead, their rate of cell division is slowed. In some types of cancer, this may mean that the tumor takes many years to develop. If for any reason the body does not react against the cancer cells, they may develop with frightening speed. This happens with some

A metaphase cell from the bone marrow of a patient with chronic myeloid leukemia (CML). The arrow indicates the abnormal chromosome.

congenital cancers which develop in the unborn child proliferating even faster than the embryo's normally rapidly dividing cells.

The scale of the problem is alarming, for cancer has now become one of the major causes of death. There may be some unavoidable reasons for the slow increase in the proportion of people contracting cancer. Cancer is largely a disease of middle and old age, when the body has passed its prime. In underdeveloped nations, where due to malnutrition or other diseases the average age at death is often not much more than thirty years old, cancer is rare. But as improved living standards increase the life span, so degenerative diseases like cancer, rheumatism and high blood pressure become more apparent. A high proportion of people dying from other causes are found at post mortem to have small tumors in their bodies. Cancer can take so long to develop that they die from unrelated causes.

In 1974, in the United States alone, 320,000 people died from cancer—twice the total American fatalities in World War II, more than five times the annual toll in road accidents, and more than a hundred times the worst recorded death rate from polio.

Our best hope of controlling cancer is to understand what causes a cell to become changed sufficiently to trigger off the explosive growth which ultimately results in a tumor. We now know that no single cause can be

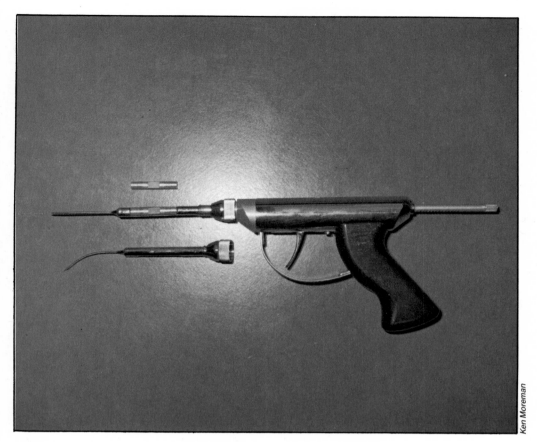

Ken Moreman

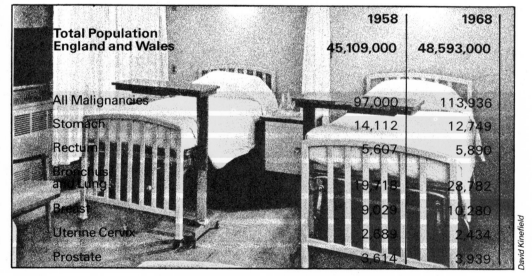

	1958	1968
Total Population England and Wales	45,109,000	48,593,000
All Malignancies	97,000	113,936
Stomach	14,112	12,749
Rectum	5,607	5,890
Bronchus and Lung	19,715	28,782
Breast	9,029	10,280
Uterine Cervix	2,689	2,434
Prostate	3,614	3,939

David Kinefield

Top: A radon gun for shooting radioactive seeds into malignant areas. Above: The comparative figures of various types of cancer over ten years in England and Wales bear out fluctuations also noted on a global scale.

found. Cancer is the result of separate and unrelated factors which can, when present at the right time, cause cells to become malignant.

Some of these factors arise within the body. Cancer cells have abnormal chromosomes, the tiny strands of genetic material which act as a blueprint for the cell. If the blueprint is damaged, the cell will produce abnormal offspring when it divides. Radioactivity and X-rays can produce chromosome breakages of this types. Long-term use of LSD has also been said to produce genetic damage, but this is a matter of controversy.

Other factors exist in our external environment. Some researchers believe that as many as 80 percent of cancers have an external environmental origin; a few feel that *all* cancer will eventually prove to be caused by external factors. The variation in type of cancer is very marked if it is studied on a global scale. By noting where and when certain types of cancer predominate, it is sometimes possible to work back and determine the cause. But a map of the world showing the relative frequency of different cancers reveals no obvious pattern. In Egypt, bladder cancer is very common. Lung cancer is more frequent in Britain than in any other country. In Iceland, half the cancers occurring in men are of the digestive system. Stomach cancer is disproportionately common in Japan. In Australia, New Zealand and South Africa, skin cancers are a major problem. What sort of pattern emerges?

By studying diet, climatic conditions, other diseases, and genetics, we can sometimes identify one factor which can complete the set of conditions necessary before a malignancy can develop. A simple analogy is to compare the precancerous state with a parked automobile in which a small child is left to play. If the child releases the handbrake, if the car is standing on a slope, if the wheel bearings are sufficiently free-running, *and* if the vehicle happens to roll into a river —*then* the damage is done.

Racial Patterns

With cancer, there may be a slight racial tendency towards developing a certain kind of tumor and, very rarely, cancer may be inherited. One particular family in the United States is a medical curiosity because of the high proportion who develop bowel cancers. A group in the community may be exposed to a stimulus which can activate cancer cells, but only if they are of the susceptible age or sex.

In very hot countries, excessive exposure to the sun is incriminated as the trigger to start off skin cancers— hence the high incidence in Australia, New Zealand and South Africa. Smoked fish is known to contain chemicals which may start cancer, which might account for a high rate of stomach cancers in Iceland and elsewhere. Bladder cancer in Egypt is known to be more likely in people infected with bilharzia, a disease caused by parasitic flukes which damage the bladder wall. Slowly but surely, factors such as these are being identified. Some of the most baffling variations may eventually yield useful conclusions. How do we explain, for instance, the high rate of skin and mouth cancer in Ireland—ten times greater than in England, although Ireland is only a few miles away?

While conditions within our bodies are not easy to control, understanding external factors offers the possibility of avoiding the disease or of making a complete cure. The most promising fields of research are into chemical causes and biological agents.

Some chemical causes of cancer, or carcinogens, have been known for many years. As long ago as 1895, cancer of the bladder occurred frequently among workers in the aniline dye industry. The substances responsible were eventually isolated and found to be used in other industries, such as rubber manufacture, and insulated cable production. Once identified, these carcinogens were controlled.

Similar examples were known even earlier. Cancer of the scrotum was common among boys who once used to clean the soot from the inside of chimneys.

Some cancers can be regarded as occupational diseases. Particular types of lung cancer are common in workers in the asbestos industry and in nickel and chromium refineries. Even woodworkers may develop cancer through continuous inhalation of wood dust. Recently workers in plants manufacturing plastics were found to be prone to develop an unusual liver cancer, caused by inhaling minute amounts of a chemical called vinyl chloride.

By the time the danger is discovered, however, it may be too late.

Chemicals in our diet cause a greater problem, as it is very difficult to prove that a suspect substance is a carcinogen. A chemical may be injected into a mouse or rat, or painted on its skin, and so cause a tumor to develop. This does not necessarily prove that the same thing will happen in man, of course, and it is never ethically acceptable to try potential carcinogens on man. Similarly, if a tumor cannot be induced in an experimental animal, the test substance is not necessarily safe; it may simply be that the time it would take for the cancer to develop is longer than the brief life span of the mouse. So we can never be certain that any substance is

A Stage towards the developments of malignant melanoma (a tumor of pigment-forming cells). Top: The multiplication of melanocytes (appearing brown) and some dipping of the epidermis. Middle: An early stage in which inflammatory cells (dark blue dots) have appeared and, right, the edge of an invasive tumor colored brown. Bottom: The full thickness of the section is replaced by nodules of melanoma cells, of which an occasional one is pigmented. A common feature of cancer is the loss of the cell's ability to function, here shown by loss of pigmentation.

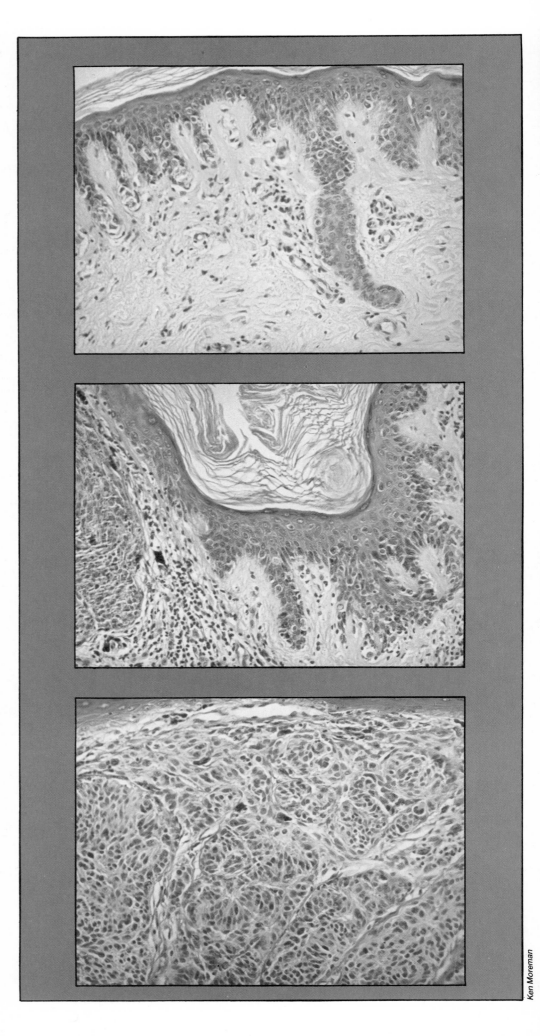

Ken Moreman

safe, or that it will cause cancer. We can rely only on probabilities.

Other potential hazards are still with us. In the 1950s, a mysterious disease caused the deaths of huge numbers of young turkeys in Britain, due to liver cancer. At about the same time, liver cancers killed off large numbers of rainbow trout in American trout farms. The trouble was traced to food pellets containing peanut meal. This was contaminated with aflatoxin, a chemical produced by molds, when the nuts were stored in damp conditions after harvesting. And in Africa and parts of Asia, where moldy peanuts are commonly eaten, there is a disproportionate amount of liver cancer in humans. It would be unrealistic not to assume that there is a close relationship.

By far the most widely accepted environmental carcinogen is the one easiest to avoid—tobacco smoke. The cause and effect are too well established to need discussion, and the problem is now mainly economic and political. No nation has yet had the courage to ban cigarette smoking totally, because of the enormous revenues collected in taxes on tobacco. The annual toll in lung cancer is tragic and largely avoidable—the risk increases in proportion to the quantity of cigarettes smoked. Substituting pipes or cigars is no solution: with them the chances of the smoker contracting cancer of the mouth and tongue are markedly increased.

Nothing to Digest

Another source of worry to Westerners is an ever-increasing number of cancers of the bowel and rectum. This is thought to result from our specialized diets. In African and Asian cultures, the largely vegetable diets contain a high proportion of indigestible fiber. This roughage means that the intestinal contents pass rapidly through the bowel, and the feces are comparatively bulky. In Western diets there is more meat, and cereal products are refined to remove fiber. Consequently almost all the food is digested, and it takes much longer for the smaller quantities of feces to pass through our systems. The result seems to be that the bacteria inhabiting the gut are present in different proportions in the bowel of Western man. The theory is that carcinogenic metabolic waste products of these bacteria may cause bowel cancer. The solution is apparently equally straightforward: eat foods containing more fiber, or add bran to your breakfast cereal.

The other major cause of cancer may well be viruses. In recent years, a wide range of cancers affecting mammals and birds have turned out to be spread by viruses, tiny particles which are incapable of growing independently but must always feed off a living cell. One virus infects the breast tissue of the female mouse and is passed to its offspring as they suckle.

There is suspicion, almost amounting to certainty, that some human cancers may have a viral origin, but unless the viruses can be seen and identified there is no likelihood of this being proved. Once more, it would be unethical to demonstrate the truth of the theory by attempting to infect another person.

Cancer by Virus

Viruses have been found in cancer cells from children suffering from Burkitt's lymphoma, a tumor of the face which usually occurs only in Africa and other tropical areas. Investigation has shown that this disease occurs only in regions where malaria is common, and it is speculated that the infection might be spread from person to person by mosquitoes.

Even cancer of the cervix, common in middle-aged women, may be an infectious disease caused by a virus. It is notably rare in nuns and other women with limited sexual experience. Conversely, it is much more common than average in prostitutes and in women who started sexual activities at an early age. This could mean that cervical cancer is a sexually transmitted venereal disease or possibly that a carcinogen may be secreted in the male's semen or from glands in the penis.

If viruses can be incriminated in causing common cancers, it is possible that vaccines could be developed to provide immunity. Failing this, there are other methods for treating established cancers. Tumors can be removed surgically, although this usually depends on finding them before they progress to secondary tumors. A few drugs are available which, together with X-ray treatment and radiation therapy, act by poisoning or weakening all the cells, in the hope that cancer cells will succumb before healthy cells. These extremely toxic substances cause tumors to regress or shrink, but they usually grow back rapidly. In the last few years, however, researchers have produced complete cures with drugs. The first to be completely cured was Burkitt's lymphoma, which can be destroyed with a single dose of a drug.

A few other rare cancers can also be treated chemically, and there has recently been a breakthrough in leukemia. This is a cancer of the white blood cells, which arises in the bone marrow. A particularly acute form is quite common in children and has proved universally fatal. But now a technique has been developed for dosing children with a series of drugs, changing to the next before serious side effects emerge, and some children have survived for years after treatment.

There may be 1,000,000,000,000 cancer cells in the blood of a leukemic child. Each dose of a drug reduces the number, but if even a *single* malignant cell remains, it could multiply to produce the original number again within a few weeks. Odd cancer cells may linger in the brain, out of reach of drugs carried in the bloodstream, so radiation treatment is used to eradicate these. In adults, leukemia is less responsive to the treatment, but encouraging results have been obtained and a few cures effected using this method.

By attacking the problem of cancer with a variety of established techniques, several forms of the disease may succumb to treatment. One new method is to encourage the body to fight back by vaccinating with BCG—inactivated tuberculosis bacteria which generally stimulate the body's immunity system. Widespread educational and screening programs are under way to encourage people to seek early treatment for symptoms that resemble those of cancer.

Unspoken Fears

Fear of the disease is so great that many women finding a lump in their breast delay going to the doctor, terrified that he may confirm they have cancer. By then, the tumor may have spread. By showing women how to examine their breasts for lumps and by encouraging routine cervical smear tests, many of these common cancers of Western civilization can be identified early enough for relatively minor surgery to be totally effective and for the cancer to be eradicated.

With a complex disease or series of diseases like cancer, it is unrealistic to anticipate a single medical breakthrough to solve the problem. But already we can avoid much of the disease by controlling our environment and diet. If the armor of fear can be penetrated enough to ensure that people seek early medical treatment, the weapons we have at the moment may prove sufficient to control most kinds of cancer.

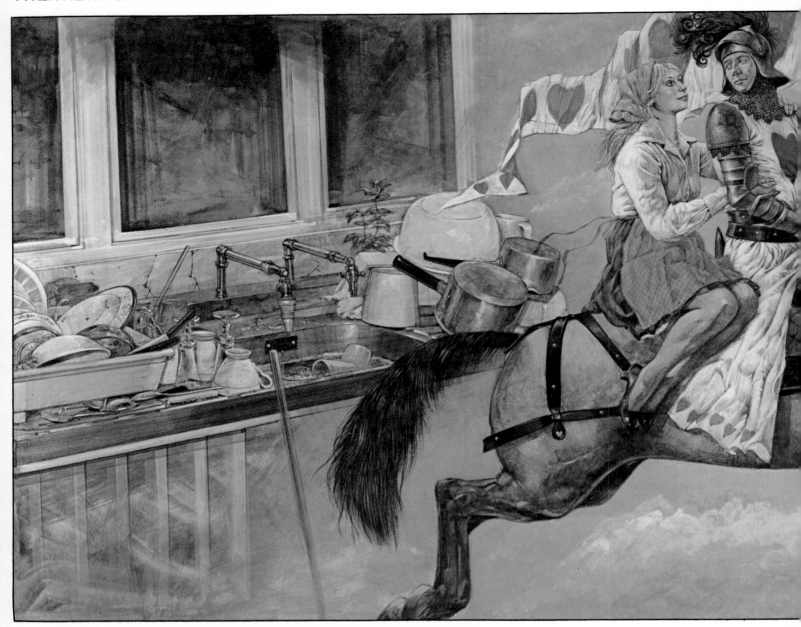

Matchmakers

Marriage bureaus will make you a match, but if you're looking for a knight in shining armor, go elsewhere. The chances are your chosen one will carry you off to the kitchen sink.

"I was shocked when I discovered how they had described me." An attractive and intelligent 33-year-old, Shirley had registered with a marriage bureau and had been disconcerted by the whole process.

"They said I was 'very pretty, petite, ash blonde—an understanding, loving nursery teacher.' It gave quite the wrong impression. I am ordinarily attractive, but I certainly can't be described as 'very pretty'—in fact I am rather overweight, so although I am only 5 foot 2, calling me 'petite' is

dodging the issue. My hair *is* fair, but having it called ash blonde made me take a fresh look at it, and I realized that it's a bit faded, now, with some gray in it. And I cannot imagine how they constructed the 'sweet-natured' or 'loving' bit, from a few minutes' conversation. In any case, I'm a university graduate, which they didn't mention, and I have got strong progressive views about education: I'm no dolly bird, whichever way you look at it."

One of the men Shirley met through the agency had been distinctly irri-

tated. "And I could sympathize with him, really," she said. "He'd been led to expect someone quite different in personality and fairly different in appearance." He had also made sexual approaches to her almost at once and had seemed surprised when she rebuffed him. "I suppose *that* wasn't really his fault, either," said Shirley. "I'm sure he interpreted my being described as 'loving'—which puzzles *me* a bit, anyway—as meaning sexually promiscuous."

The agency's need to falsify her

Richard Hook

description not only made her feel a cheat: she felt a physical failure. "For a time afterwards I quite uncharacteristically felt old and faded and virtually unlovable. I consoled myself with the thought that the men's descriptions also made *them* sound more desirable than they were, but of course less emphasis is placed on a man's physical appearance, so the discrepancies are not so immediately obvious when a meeting takes place."

Like all agencies, marriage bureaus benefit by overstating the value of their "product." Employment agencies and accommodation agencies do the same thing: the "highly desirable home in a fashionable area" rarely turns out to be very desirable; the "experienced secretary with high speeds" may be inexperienced and slow. Agency interviews often affect unbounded enthusiasm for the particular product on offer, in the not

unjustified hope that sometimes the client will be carried along by this sentiment and ignore the discrepancy between the trade description and the reality.

One man's marriage agency expressed great personal happiness at the perfect match they had found him. It was "one of the best matches we have ever achieved" they told him joyfully. When the meeting took place, however, he was exasperated. His "perfect match" was unattractive, she towered over him, and she talked endlessly about herself and her work.

Chalk and Cheese
This "perfect match" was certainly unrealistic on the agency's part—the difference in height preempted the possibility of compatibility—but the man was also unrealistic. He was a poor conversationalist and one reason that his date talked endlessly may

have been to fill in the awkward silences. There was also the possibility, which he also seemed not to consider, that her nervousness took the form of garrulousness, whereas his made him taciturn.

It is difficult enough for two strangers to relate to each other at a first meeting, whether or not they turn out to be well-matched. The most common reported fault is mutual unresponsiveness. Each partner depends on the agency's matching methods to make the meeting easy, regarding the chosen partner as a sort of gift designed exactly to their needs, whether their need is for an entertaining companion who will shoulder all the contact responsibilities or for an eager listener. Some agencies recognize this common habit of unresponsiveness and exhort their clients, "When you meet, make an effort to *be* interesting and to *show* interest."

If a woman is passive or has poor social skills, it does not make much difference whether she enrolls with a computer-dating agency or with a marriage bureau. But a man who is passive or awkward is more likely to use the latter. A computer agency will expect him to telephone unknown females and to ask for a date, whereas a marriage bureau will arrange an introduction for him. Marriage widowhood. However one great advance in the marriage-bureau market is that single mothers are now offered without embarrassment or apology.

Charming Idiom

Marriage bureaus are prone to a curiously old-fashioned method of describing their clients. Computer agencies, however, with their affection for psychosocial jargon, do at least sound a part of the 1970s. Even so, one bureau concocted a description of a woman client that makes it difficult to see what sort of man she might attract—apart from a sexually disturbed one. The description read: "Ruth is 38, but looks younger. She is tall with lovely long black hair hanging over her shoulders, a dark complexion, black eyes, and her own teeth. . . . She comes from a good family. She doesn't drink, smoke or gamble. She had a boyfriend for a long time but always kept pure. One evening she was drugged by him and he had intercourse with her without her knowledge. It was a shock to her and she saw him no more. This one sad act made her pregnant. . . . Ruth speaks beautifully, likes music . . . and would be a wonderful partner to a suitable gentleman who loves children."

In advertisements listing the charms of their current clients it is usual for bureaus to use most of the space describing the client, with only a few words describing the sort of partner sought. The largest of the London marriage bureaus frequently describes its male clients as loyal, rather shy, patient, kind, cheerful, polite, amiable, and even placid. These are defensive-sounding qualities that seem to indicate some bewilderment or hurt in the man's past treatment at the hands of women—and a consequent reluctance to risk emotional commitment. They

The heart is a lonely hunter. The world is full of desolate people looking for someone to love. Lonely hearts clubs hold out the promise of bringing together all those seeking a life partner and helping them to make a match.

are often divorced or have reached their late thirties without marrying. They are often successful in their occupations and own not only a car and a house but a boat. Their failure is in social relationships. The woman they would like to meet is usually essentially undemanding: home-loving, understanding, quiet, cheerful, sweet-natured and, again, loyal. The men described sound rather convalescent, with their desired woman having the matronly qualities of a convalescent's housekeeper.

Unlike computer-dating services, marriage bureaus have a long past, catering for a number of people "over 39" and so tending to retain an old-fashioned vocabulary. But it is curious that they are not aware of the untempt-

ingly passive picture they present of their male clients. The repetition of the same words throughout many advertisements indicates that the choice of words is the agency's rather than the client's, even though the client does contribute. When asked "Would you describe yourself as 'high-powered, active, or placid?'" the wise client refutes their choice of words and offers one of his own.

Pretty Materialistic

The bureau's women clients are rather differently described, with emphasis on appearance rather than occupation. Women are presented as beautiful, pretty or "captivating"; they may have a "bubbly personality" or be "vivacious." They seem briskly

David Lewis

materialistic about the man they seek, often specifying that a prospective mate own a car or house and that he be "financially secure" or have "comfortable assets." In character he is not usually the undynamic, avuncular male so frequently on offer by the agency, however; in fact, some women ask for a "strong personality." Where a "kindly" or "patient" man *is* specified, it is usually because the woman has been left with children to bring up alone, through divorce or widowhood. However one great advance in the marriage-bureau market is that single mothers are now offered without embarrassment or apology.

Comfortably Off

Women on the bureau's books are sometimes financially comfortable: they have been divorced or widowed and have a house or a car, or perhaps even a business. Perhaps they have never married, because of an occupation they enjoyed and have had time to acquire possessions but not friends. Jenny, a 29-year-old research chemist, is a typical case. "I was busy advancing my career, I suppose," she said, "and acquiring possessions—which gave me great pleasure. Then a year or two ago I began to realize that my life-style was not bringing me in touch with unattached men very often and that my social life would become increasingly limited unless I did something about it. All my friends had married, and I became very conscious of how couple-oriented the world is."

People using marriage bureaus may seem socially desirable, not only well endowed with worldly goods but also educated. There are, for example, bureaus confining themselves to university graduates or professional people—"if you are choosy about the company you keep."

Financial and educational achievement does not, however, ensure self-confidence. Both men and women sometimes opt out of an arranged meeting, either concealing themselves at the meeting place or consenting to an exchange of letters or phone calls with the arranged partner but postponing an actual meeting.

Women in particular are sometimes reported to relish receiving and replying to letters from a man with whom the bureau has put her in touch, and yet persistently avoid a meeting. For her, writing letters at leisure and looking forward to receiving the answers is a comforting and stimulating activity, full of hope but with little risk of disillusionment.

Such women might be deemed

Marshall Cavendish

better off with another established institution, the correspondence club. This is a favorite method of cheating the customer, however: organizations purporting to be correspondence clubs are likely to operate from a box number or an accommodation address, and they request money in advance. Having sent off the money, the customer often never hears anything more from them. There is a higher failure rate in correspondence clubs than in any other kind.

Making Contact

Contact clubs have become big business. The social and geographical mobility of modern society creates many lonely people, and modern medical care has created great numbers of active retired and semiretired people with many years of unaccustomed leisure in front of them. Most of the clubs are run for gain; a few are non-profit-making—but not very many.

There are lonely hearts clubs for the young and for the old, for the privileged and underprivileged, for people with an interest in common, and for people with no interests to speak of. They also operate for that increasingly large section of the popu-

Now let's see who we have here: someone suitable to squire a divorced lady who likes to read? How about a skin-diving accountant with no preferences or perhaps a young lawyer with thespian tendencies? That will be $50, if you please.

lation, the divorced, the separated, the widowed, or the unmarried.

For the middle-aged and elderly, perhaps the best sort of contact club is the ballroom dancing school. Here the clients get rhythmic exercise, along with music and conversation. And there is also the element of body contact—lonely widowed or divorced people, perhaps long deprived of any physical communication, move into each other's arms and sweep off together to the sort of music they find warming and stimulating. It is remarkable that this quaintly old-fashioned area of life should so well provide the physical contact that is part of modern encounter groups and other popular types of psychotherapy, whereas current styles of dancing have dispensed with touching altogether.

Encounter groups are on the whole more powerful in their effect than most other types of contact club. They challenge the member's self-concept and experiment—at some risk—with methods of breaking down his customary defense mechanisms. Mentally disturbed people are attracted to such activities, both as members and as group directors, and harm can result. Such groups can be beneficial where meetings are conducted under competent supervision and where someone who has been disturbed by a meeting is kept in touch with afterwards. But many people find these groups too immediately challenging and unpleasantly aggressive.

There is sometimes a strong element of sexual stimulation in certain encounter groups, including nudity, group body massage, and some overt sexual activity. A group with such a reputation will attract sexually disturbed people, or sexually unscrupulous people, and harm may result.

The entire contact industry is prone to attract people who are seeking only sexual experiences. There are great numbers of clubs promoting this, of course. Local legal conditions dictate the frankness or covertness of their operation, and it is often done under cover of an apparently ordinary contact club.

An eighteenth century marriage market. Once upon a time marriages between people of wealth or property were usually arranged. They were regarded as business mergers.

Mary Evans

To exclude sexually predatory people, a genuine club has to be careful how it words its advertisements, as sexual connotations may be inferred from many seemingly innocent phrases. The sexual underworld has an extensive vocabulary that is, they claim, instantly recognizable by any of their kind. One club for transvestites and transsexuals had a "shop" of women's clothing in the clubroom, the chief club activity being to watch each other try on these clothes in front of a huge mirror. The club organizer regularly placed advertisements in a general weekly paper offering "lovely clothes for young women, all sizes and styles, hardly worn" and maintained that they never received answers from "straights" but always from transvestites.

Their assumption that sexual deviants recognized their seemingly innocuous advertisement for what it was is not so important; but it is unfortunate that they assumed that innocents also recognized it. It is this assumption that leads to countless damaging encounters in the aboveboard contact industry. The sexual predator or deviant refuses to believe that everybody does not see sexual connotations wherever he sees them.

Many clubs for deviants are minor operations, conducted from the organizer's living room as a spare-time activity. Legitimate contact clubs are often so operated, and, on the whole, small local clubs provide more viable contacts than large central organizations.

Like-minded People

One recent type of small contact club with big hopes aims to foster interaction between like-minded people living in the same area, introduced to each other by the central organization. It is not specifically intended to be a lonely hearts club but often works in that way. There is no club meeting place: they meet at each other's homes. The central organization recruits the members and takes their membership fees, and then puts them in touch with a group meeting in their area. It is an inexpensively run operation, leaving the organization of meeting to the members themselves.

Many contact clubs, especially such loosely structured ones, suffer from frequently cancelled meetings. Encounter groups, for example, are notorious for planning ambitious-sounding meetings and exhorting people to attend and then finding it suddenly inconvenient to hold them,

often because the response is poor and it would be financially unprofitable in their view. Also, a club may proffer an interesting calendar of frequent events to a prospective member but fail to reveal that half of them are usually cancelled.

Any club that caters for the isolated has a large proportion of people who never achieve real communication with any other member. When the club has failed to produce the ideal partner or friends, it is treated merely as a place to go. "The club isn't much good, really, but anything is better than sitting in your room by yourself" is how it was summed up by one member. He found it difficult to make friends and impossible to form lasting relationships with women, but he had not attempted to alter his passive, unresponsive attitude towards people. He felt that he had done everything that could reasonably be expected of him merely by joining something.

Going it Alone

The clubs for the divorced, separated and widowed vary according to their organizers. Some people find it depressing to be in the company of people who have all been deprived of a life partner. But women tend to find it more reassuring, because in our society unattached women approaching middle age are made to feel helpless outsiders. A man, who is allowed to take the initiative in intersexual encounters, has more expansive means of acquiring partners and is in any case a more desirable social commodity than the single woman of comparable age. There are also many more widows than widowers, because a woman's life span is longer than a man's at present. For these various reasons there tends to be a shortage of men in such clubs: one club organizing a dinner dance had to resort to a male-escort service to make up the number of men.

Like any other organization, clubs for the divorced or separated contain many people whose established social habits are disagreeable, but who refuse to acknowledge the need to learn new ones. There is often a hard core of embittered people, endlessly airing their sense of hurt about the treatment they have received at the hands of their past partners. For these, long use of such a club reinforces their social inadequacy rather than helping them recover from the trauma of losing a life partner. But there are many people who are able to make good use of the organizations and clubs prepared to help them find a friend.

Ron Embleton

Con artist?

Does the man with a message need a PR mouthpiece to get across to the man in the street?

"PR Department, Abolition of." So runs the title of the section on public relations in *Up The Organization*, the distillation of Robert Townsend's experience as whizkid chairman of the Avis Rent-a-Car Corporation. After recommending "fire the whole advertising department and your old agency" and "fire the whole personnel department," he goes on to PR. "Yes, fire this whole department. If you have an outside PR firm, fire them too." "Most businesses," he adds, "have a normal PR operation: press releases, clipping services, attempts to get interviewed, all being handled as usual by people who are embarrassingly uninformed about the company's plans and objectives."

He may, of course, be right. Perhaps whole PR departments should be fired. Indeed, some might say the whole PR business ought to be dismantled. But, for all his short-term success with Avis (which now has PR departments and uses outside consultants), Townsend stands condemned out of his own mouth. Though his conclusions may be correct, his arguments betray in him the very embarrassing lack of information that he is attributing to others, for to think of PR merely as "press releases, clipping services, attempts to get interviewed . . ." indicates a degree of incomprehension surprising in the head of a major company, but by no means untypical.

All Things to All Men

One of the most common complaints of PR practitioners is that, since their profession is so often misunderstood, its skills are usually inadequately or improperly applied—which increases the chances of being misunderstood. It is important to ask, "If the PR department is apparently not doing its job properly, does the fault lie in the nature of PR or in the way it is being used (or misused)?" And to answer that fundamental question, it is necessary to know what the job of PR is in the first place.

According to the bland definition coined by the Institute of Public Relations, the job of PR is "to establish and maintain mutual understanding between organizations and their publics [PR jargon for the groups of people you want to influence] by means of deliberate, planned and sustained efforts." The problem is that "mutual understanding" means all things to all people and consequently ceases to have any real meaning. And since the Institute is apparently unable to find a meaningful definition of its members' activities, the uninitiated can be forgiven for not understanding it either. However, the problem is further complicated by the fact that, since the Institute speaks for its members and is run by practicing PR men, members themselves either do not know or cannot agree what PR really is.

The diversity of opinion within the PR industry itself, the misconceptions held by those who employ PR men and consequently do so for the wrong reasons, and the professional vulnerability of the PR men themselves which makes them unwilling to stand up to clients or employers adds up to a confusing picture and one that induces suspicion and mistrust in the lay public. Include the more bizarre notions about PR men—that they exist at worst to procure call girls for visiting customers and at best to be a front for shady operations—and it is small wonder that the image of the image builders is so tarnished.

As a consequence of this poor reputation, deserved or not, in the last few years PR men have taken to describing their business as "communications." But, although the term may have fewer pejorative overtones than "public relations," it actually broadens a definition that is already too broad and only creates still more confusion. A certain multinational corporation with a base in London had, until recently when it took Townsend's advice to heart, an "International Coordinator, Communications," who not only ran the PR department but handled bookings for the company's jet as well.

As far as definitions of PR go, Richard Kirsch was probably not too far off the mark when he said in *The Private Life of Public Relations* that PR men exist to "service and exploit the existing and continuously expanding web of contact and communications." And it is through this network that politicians and civil servants manage public affairs and through which businessmen manage industry. However, when a PR man talks about "communication," he probably means "influence" or "persuasion." It is, then, the job of PR men to exploit the channels of communication between those who employ their services and the objects of the persuasion. Apart from specialist activities like government propaganda and fund raising for charities, political campaigns and protest groups, most exploitation of communications systems is undertaken on behalf of commercial enterprises.

Any commercial organization will, at one time or another, want to exert influence on other key groups—notably customers (trade or public), employees (present and potential), stockholders and financial institutions, and government and official bodies. Since these groups between them cover most aspects of commercial activity, the PR man's professional arena is vast. As a result, while most practitioners profess a general grasp of the whole range of activities, they will tend to specialize in one area and seek extra specialist help as required.

Too Little, Too Late

Few industrial companies can afford (nor do they need) to employ, full-time, enough PR staff to cover the whole spectrum. Normal practice is to have a small PR department or a resident press information officer for day-to-day operations and to call in an agency which can be expected to supply the appropriate specialists for whatever length of time they are needed. Despite the obvious economic advantages of this sort of approach, it is all too often true that, though specialist advice is needed in the earliest planning stages of any PR exercise, most companies will put off hiring outside help until the last possible minute in the hope of shaving a few percent off the final bill. In retrospect, this invariably turns out to be a false economy.

One of the stories told most frequently by PR men to illustrate a similar point concerns a giant dam built across a valley and towering over half a dozen picturesque villages. One day, the watchman hears an ominous creaking sound and, looking out of his office window, sees a small crack appear in the wall of the dam. As he reaches for the telephone, the crack widens and the trickle becomes a torrent. On the verge of panic he gets through to the Water Board switchboard and cries, "Quick, put me through to public relations." Far too often, the PR man is called in only when it is too late.

On Target

For "communications," as for any other management function, the sequence of events should begin with the definition of broad objectives, short- and long-term. From this is distilled the message that has to be put across, be it "buy this product" or "invest in this company" or "we are a good company to work for." Then the target publics must be precisely identified (far too much time and money are thrown away attempting to influence people who cannot help in achieving the objective). When that has been done, an overall communications strategy can be prepared, which will decide which channels of communication, which media, will be used and how. Ideally, specialists from marketing (including advertising), financial and government relations should cooperate in establishing the master plan not only to produce a coherent package but to prevent later conflicts of interest and all-round confusion.

Far too often companies start off with an idea for a communications tool—a company brochure, for example, or a press conference, or a sales conference, or a circular to stockholders, or a house journal—and work backwards, until they discover a strategy that will justify it. Here, objectives are born out of tactics, something which, though nonsensical in any situation, tends to be the rule rather than the exception in the PR business. The proper sequence of events is objectives: message: publics: media.

The relative importance of the four

key PR areas—customer (marketing PR), employee, financial and government relations—varies according to the nature of the enterprise and the objectives which its communications strategy has to meet. But it is in the marketing area where the vast majority of PR work is undertaken. Ideally the activities of the PR men should go hand in hand with those of their advertising colleagues, for the object of the exercise is more often than not to achieve favorable publicity for a product or service as part of an overall promotional campaign. While it is generally accepted that advertising is the main *selling* tool, its efforts can often be neutralized if public opinion is negative. Or, put the other way around, it helps if an advertising campaign is set against a background of favorable comment and opinion.

At the same time, it is also generally accepted that people are more readily influenced by what they read or hear in the editorial matter of the media, believing the information to be more reliable and objective, than by ads, which do not have the same degree of credibility. Furthermore, it has been estimated that at least twice as many people read the editorial matter of newspapers and magazines as look at the ads. It is for these reasons that a new improved form of publicity is beginning to spring up, known as "sponsored editorials."

These abound in certain mass-circulation fashion magazines, where manufacturers pay directly for their products to be mentioned in glowing terms in editorial features, accompanied by suitable photographs. This system works out very much cheaper than straight advertising and probably has considerably greater impact. Protestations from other journals that such a practice is contrary to the spirit of the Code of Advertising Practice are taken with a grain of salt. Often, all that is happening is that journalists are being paid in cash rather than in free trips, champagne and smoked salmon for writing the same story.

For all that, there are relatively few instances where the influence of PR on sales can actually be measured. The launch of a new product or service offers an opportunity for precise measurement of the success of indivual promotion methods, but it is usually accompanied by both PR and advertising and it is usually impossible to gauge the relative efficiency of the

An exciting world of sport is open to smokers of Classic cigarettes—at least so says the PR man.

two. It is only when PR operates on its own that its effect can be measured, but all the experts advise against using PR alone, claiming greatest effectiveness when it is an integral part of the marketing mix, at the same time ensuring that PR's ineffectiveness cannot be shown up.

However, small companies like certain fashion houses, unable to afford a large advertising budget, have launched their new products very successfully using only PR. It is here that either the PR man's media contacts or his skill at staging a newsworthy event becomes of great importance, for if publicity cannot be bought, it has to be created. For most purposes, PR

men are content to supply journalists, particularly those working in the lower echelons of trade magazines, with large quantities of food and drink to achieve favorable publicity for any particular event. But there still remains a handful of journalists in the national press and in high-circulation glossy magazines who are harder to woo, feeling that their readers are entitled to something that can at least be passed off as news, however thinly this disguises the PR content of the eventual write-up. For the budding PRO it is as well to keep this in mind, since clients and employees are more impressed at seeing their names and products in the nationals and glossies

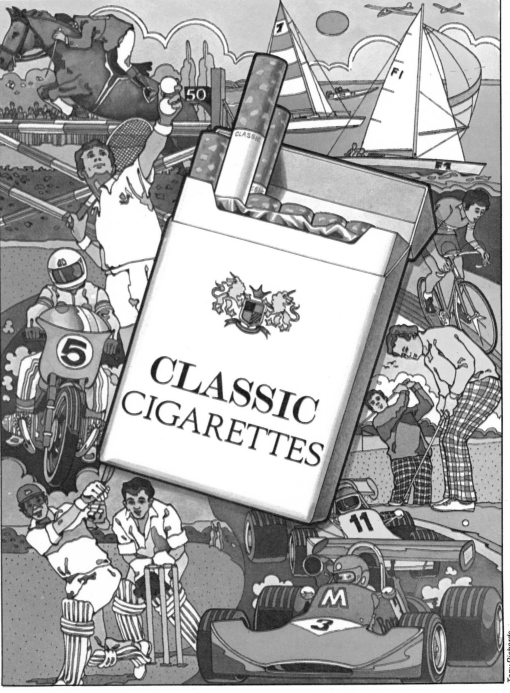

Tony Richards

than in trade magazines—despite the fact that it is in trade magazines that mentions are often more effective. Many clients and PR men still measure their effectiveness in column inches.

Public Image

The promotion of show business personalities gave the PR man new material for his act. In the heyday of Hollywood when there was a direct and easy equation between publicity, popularity and success—irrespective of talent—the most successful PR men were those who could dream up the most spectacular and newsworthy events for their clients. Contemporary observers lost count of the number of "children saved from drowning" by starlets, not to mention the plethora of scandalous incidents, all carefully stage-managed—anything indeed that could make a front-page headline.

Personality PR of this sort is now applied as much on behalf of company chairmen as it used to be on starlets. Indeed, as Daniel Boorstin observed in *The Image*, "Shakespeare, in the familiar lines, divided great men into three classes: those born great, those who achieve greatness and those who have greatness thrust upon them. It never occurred to him to mention those who hire relations experts to make themselves look great."

In the business world, marketing PR operates on two distinct but not separate levels—consumer and trade. National media are simply not interested in writing glowing reports on mass-produced consumer products like chocolate bars or washing powder. So effective PR for such items in these media doesn't stand a chance. The only time products of this sort become newsworthy is when there is something wrong with them.

However, while mass advertising is better able to take care of the consumer in this instance, the manufacturer's relations with the trade (wholesalers and retailers) are still of great importance, since, if they do not stock his goods, no amount of advertising will help. So far as PR within the trade is concerned, the only limiting factor is money. And the job is effective in proportion to its creativeness. But since trade journals are often hungry for material anyway, not being able to afford large staffs of reporters to track down news, they are often grateful for stories from public relations offices, providing they are tolerably newsworthy.

Some companies even go so far as to publish their own journals for distribution to the trade, with details of trade deals, special offers, and the like. Others sponsor competitions—a large manufacturer of electrical goods provides an annual week's golfing at an exclusive Majorca country club for wholesalers who purchase more than a certain quantity of goods.

In Britain it is extremely difficult to achieve favorable publicity for mass-produced consumer products in the national press and on television, which is not as dominated by advertising as American television is. The cost of staging an event for a mass consumer product that will be newsworthy enough to achieve a favorable mention in these media is so prohibitive (unless it happens by chance) that it is no longer undertaken except in certain specialist areas like travel, show business, and fashion.

Sporting Chance

Perhaps the only cast-iron way of getting company names or brand names mentioned in the leading media in any sort of gratuitously favorable way is through sports sponsorship. While sponsored sports events provide an opportunity to keep names in the public eye, to polish the company image by being associated with something wholesome, to wine and dine customers, to meet the press and to throw a jamboree for employees, it is still difficult to justify in terms of cash returns. Nevertheless, they provide a much needed source of backing for sporting events and can be justified in terms of prestige advertising. But, although it is appropriate for manufacturers of sporting equipment to sponsor such events and although there is a certain corny logic in a cigarette manufacturer's hope, by sponsoring healthy activities, to offset the belief that tobacco kills, there is still too much sponsorship undertaken because a certain recreation happens to be the chairman's hobby.

On the question of employee relations, it is sometimes difficult to know where employee communications break off and industrial relations begin. So far as this branch of PR is concerned, communications is the key word. Consequently the mainstay of this speciality is the house journal, designed to make employees feel "part of the family." Here again, the temptation is to use the house journal as a vehicle for the chairman.

Money Talks

Financial PR is perhaps the most complicated area and the one that demands the most knowledge and skill. It is also an area where it is comparatively easy to gauge the effectiveness of the job PR is doing. In a takeover battle, for example, the right sort of press campaign can make a substantial and identifiable difference to the share price. On a more mundane level, there are stockholders to mollify with favorable reports about their company's performance. Meanwhile, insurance companies with financial products to sell are highly susceptible to fluctuations in public opinion. The merest suggestion that an insurance company is in trouble could precipitate a disaster.

It is also in this area that the chairman's photograph and even his more turgid pronouncements can have some effect, providing it is part of an overall campaign designed to establish his credibility to stockholders and security analysts. Indeed, discreetly ensuring that security analysts have the right information at the right time in the right way is one of the financial PR practitioner's key roles.

The question of whether the world would be better off without public relations is actually irrelevant. The fact is that anyone engaged in commerce or public life is bound to want to persuade the people he is in contact with of something at some time. And, as mechanics of the channels of communications, PR men are no more or less expendable than anyone else who operates an existing machine. What is, however, open to question, is the degree of professional skill required and the caliber of the PR practitioners.

Traditionally, the PR business has done a poor PR job on itself. Efforts to rectify the situation, to make PR respectable and to give it professional status equal to lawyers or accountants have proved ineffective. The chief reason for this state of affairs continuing is that the Institute of Public Relations and other equivalent bodies have so far been unable to identify any cohesive set of skills that would justify it. They have created a code of practice and they have established an academic syllabus with examinations leading to membership of the Institute.

While a degree of creativity is sometimes required, and a certain flair for dreaming up newsworthy events is an asset, the ability to organize and to string words together is the only essential skill—and it is easily learned. Much of the rest of what passes for skill is either pure window dressing or dependent on personal contact lubricated with lavish entertainment. Or, as one cynic recently observed of the PR business, "There's less in this than meets the eye."

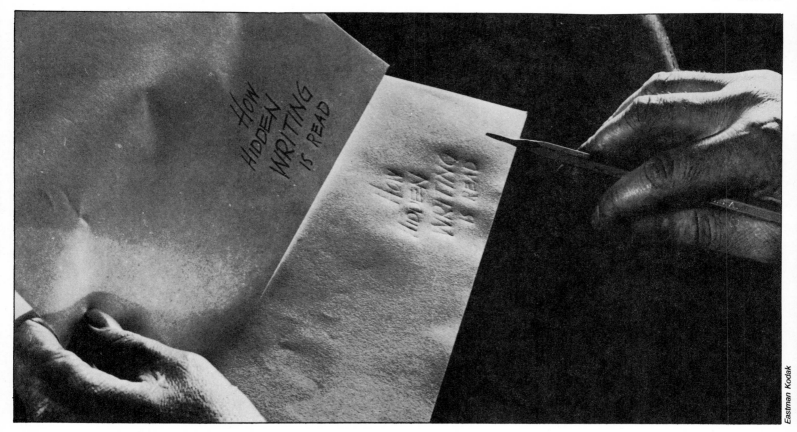

Tell-tale traces

Crime will out when the man with the microscope is on the track.

Solving a crime is one of the most demanding and satisfying puzzles a man can set his mind to, as countless murder mystery addicts will attest.

And nowhere is this kind of problem solving done with more cunning and ingenuity than in the laboratory of the forensic scientist, the expert who uses his skill and technical knowledge—and wits—to unravel legal mysteries involving anything from forgery to murder. Compared with the methods used on today's cases, Sherlock Holmes' efforts were, in his own words, elementary.

It was a saying of the French criminologist Professor Edmond Locard, one of the greatest forensic scientists of the twentieth century, that everything a man does leaves traces. But when a man tries to alter those traces he is in trouble.

Documents are so much the basis of modern life that they are obviously often involved in crimes. Documentary evidence does not mean forgery alone; the document examiner covers, both figuratively and literally, a large amount of territory.

Paper, the root of most of his work, is, to be briefly technical, an aqueous deposit of any vegetable fiber in sheet form. The name, as most people know, comes from the Latin *papyrus*, which in the hands of the early Egyptians, its first known users, comprised the pith of a sedgelike plant which was sliced into layers and beaten into sheets.

Devilish Cunning . . .

But, as so often happens, the Chinese were ahead of everybody and nearly 2000 years ago were using paper made by hand, fashioned by processes used all over the world until not long ago—though paper, as such, did not appear in Europe until about the eleventh century. In Britain paper first came from a paper mill erected around 1490; its products in fact were used for an edition of Chaucer's *Canterbury Tales*.

The forger, in his efforts to defeat science, has tried his hand at artificially aging paper. For example, the general discoloration due to age is a process of oxidation, which is easily confirmed by the expert examiner. The

faker tries to imitate this, using liquids like coffee or tea, woodfire smoke, extract of tobacco, and even permanganate of potash to achieve the vital faint brown effect.

Aging is also attempted by pressing a false document into folds and rubbing these edges along a carpet or an old wall to simulate an ancient crease. But the microscope will pick out in seconds the rubbing or dirt grains along a bogus fold.

Watermarks, another weapon of forgers, were first used in Italy about the thirteenth century. They are made when paper is a wet pulp. A dandy roll, a woven wire gauze-covered skeleton roll, has the watermark device soldered on to it. The impression of the roll on the wet pulp causes a thinning of fibers which, when the paper is finished, results in the watermark.

A faker's trick is to process finished paper by imprinting with his own dandy roll, using some sort of oily substance as a watermark; this looks genuine to the casual eye. But test it with a damp cloth or a paintbrush soaked in solvent and it vanishes.

A document cannot always be cut, marked, or touched with reagents —chemicals which act in certain ways on materials. Suppose it is important to find out if a paper contains linen and cotton, in order to date it. If it is touched with something called zinc-chlor-iodine, the marked spot will turn wine red, unthinkable on what may be a valuable document.

It is here that the microscope steps in. Dates of paper origins are generally well authenticated and if an old type of paper is examined—say, one made from rags—the linen or cotton fibers in it show features which are absolutely different from modern wood pulp papers. But—and here is the exception—many high-grade modern papers are still made from linen or cotton.

There was the case of a questioned document, brilliantly forged as it turned out. It was supposed to be 400 years old. The false writing was almost foolproof; the forger had found some old paper of the right age; and the ink used was genuine carbon ink which goes back, according to the great Egyptologist Professor Flinders Petrie, to Egypt 5,000 years ago.

The expert working on this document saw hours of investigation ahead to produce evidence that would stand up in court about something he only "felt" was wrong. Then, through his microscope ocular, he saw something incredible. Embedded in the ink of a letter was an almost invisible particle that looked metallic. Elaborate examination showed that there *were* minute particles embedded in that ink— aluminium.

This modern metal was the giveaway, for the police were later able to show that the forger's brother, working in the same room during the actual writing, was filing an aluminum casing. Aluminum dust, floating invisible in air, settled in that carefully processed carbon ink writing until the microscope found the answer.

Inks, next to paper, are usually the expert's friend. When a letter is written in ordinary ink and not blotted, it seems natural to the naked eye. A simple magnifying glass will reveal clues. If the writer paused for a second to think of a word, the lens shows the

The microscope's invention magnified the criminal's chance of apprehension. Under its all-seeing eye, typewritten text can give away as much as a hand-written signature, and evidence can still be pieced together from a scrap of paper half-dissolved in acid.

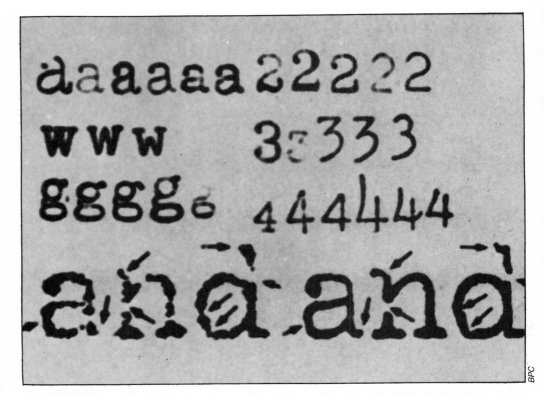

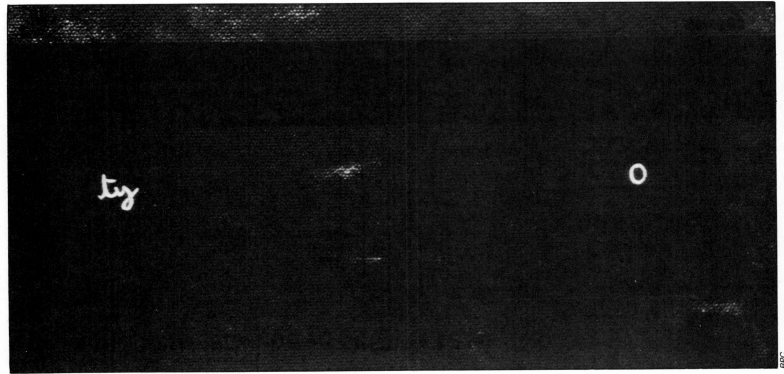

Simple addition can cause a lot of trouble when done with fraudulent intent. Here infrared light shows how to check the conversion of £7 to £70.

faintest difference in ink shading and density. Perhaps the pen lifted in the middle of a letter and then carried on.

Ink itself will "talk." One notable forensic chemist in the 1920s claimed that ink in ancient times was made from soot taken from cooking vessels, which accounts for its almost indefinite life. Iron gall ink (a mixture of ferrous sulphate with an infusion of nuts, galls and gum) came in about the first century of the Christian era. The Romans generally used an iron compound ink.

So the dating goes on—iron gall ink had logwood put into it in the middle of the eighteenth century to improve its color. A hundred years later they were using logwood with potassium chromate, and no iron, for writing purposes. All this and more means reasonably accurate dating.

The first modern ink, aniline dye ink, came in a blue form in 1861, a fairly impermanent writing fluid. This was followed by a famous advertisement for blue-black ink which showed a large blot, dark in the center, and light at the edges. Indeed it was incorrect, for in practice the reverse order would have been the case.

Nowadays, that well-known enemy of all who love good handwriting, the ball-point pen, contains a so-called solid ink which is, in fact, a thick suspension of dye in a drying oil. Its stable companion, the fiber-tipped pen, is one that, unluckily, does present problems in the forensic examination of documents.

Traces of metal, usually iron, can be found when ordinary pen marks have been erased or bleached out. Ultraviolet light will reveal these interferences. Pencils or ball-point pens often leave no residue which can be picked up after erasure, but embossing occurs in the paper used; fibers are disturbed in the paper as well, and these will answer to the expert.

The fiber-tipped pen is so light in its effect that it leaves behind no clue after erasure—other than disturbed sizing on the paper. But where additions or amendments have been made on a document written entirely with a fiber-tipped pen, then all is well —close examination soon reveals the differences in ink quality, shading and such.

Pen Names

The copying pencil, the one which leaves mauve marks on the tongue when it is accidentally licked, can be a godsend to the document examiner. In the Southampton garage murder in England in 1930, a man named Messiter was found killed; there were no apparent clues until a sharp-eyed detective picked up a dirty little scrap of paper. The back was a lodging house receipt, the front also seemed to bear words—but they were invisible under tread marks, dirt, and oil.

A simple method worked this time. The paper was very delicately washed in benzene and there, under the dirt, was the name "F. Thomas" written in copying pencil. A letter was found in the victim's files bearing this name, later proved to be an alias of a man named Podmore. It was not long before evidence was found to support a charge of murder. Podmore was duly convicted, the scrap of paper becoming vital court evidence.

Erasures continually arise in document examination. Erasures are, simply, the removal of words, often by bleaching them out before substitution. Such partial interference with documents is a common crime.

A first test is to hold the suspect document at an angle before a good light. The eye, or a magnifying glass, often reveals interference—chemical erasures tend to stand out, particularly those on paper with a high finish.

Suppose a word has been bleached out and another put in its place. The original word can generally be read by using ultraviolet light with the correct plate and filter. This method shows up the original disturbed fibers of the paper, assuming an ordinary pen has been used, and a shadow of the original word is revealed.

One of the most delicate and adroit recovery methods is one used by the late Paul Kirk, a leading American documentary expert. To recover erasures, obliterations, or indented ("ghost") writing, he used plastic casts, a process so exacting and so difficult that an ordinary man would not have patience to try it. Kirk, however, achieved some excellent results.

Burning a document is not always a successful evasion. One man in a crime burned a vital check in a grate and broke up the ashes. Experts worked for hours, spraying the fragments with diluted lacquer until they were strong enough to be touched.

Then the bits—they were no more —were reassembled until they were almost complete. Strong oblique light showed up the inked writing, which had carbonized, and the case was solved. The point of these examples is that the expert is a trained man who never neglects anything, no matter how trivial or even silly it may seem, and who possesses patience so limitless that it appears superhuman.

Another facet of document examination is graphology. This is a suspect word, for it suggests people who profess to read character from handwriting. To some extent this may be possible, but it is seldom taken seriously.

Once, at a court hearing, the writer of a letter was designated by a so-called graphologist (*not* a handwriting expert) as "French, middle-class, and young." When the man in question was called as a witness, he turned out to be the English son of an Armenian father, educated in the United States, and well over 50.

Written Evidence

But handwriting can turn out to be dangerous for the criminal when the expert deals with it. Writing, after all, is the conditioned reflex of a person using a writing instrument, and to disguise one's natural *self* in such circumstances is extremely difficult.

For example, in 1970 a great controversy raged when a British journal, *The Criminologist*, published an article which indicated that the Duke of Clarence, Queen Victoria's grandson and, until his death, heir to the English throne, might have been Jack the Ripper—the sex murderer who terrorized London's East End in 1888.

The journal itself later put an end to all this excitement by asking Professor C. L. Wilson, a document examiner in government service, to study the handwriting of the Duke and the handwritings ascribed to the "Ripper."

Professor Wilson wrote: "On the basis of the handwriting, all the evidence is against identification of Jack the Ripper with the Duke of Clarence."

Nor is the typewriter proof against the expert. The wear, the defects, the individualities of each machine all mean something to the expert, who, given a sample, can produce all sorts of vital facts. The magnifying glass, the microscope, and measuring devices play their part in studying wear, defects, accidentals (dirt, damaged letters, and so on).

The slant of the characters, angles, alignment, and footing are important —footing being that a letter may strike heavier on right, left, or bottom.

Every typewriter is peculiar to itself, after a little use. Similarity in all details in two machines may be ignored (the chance of complete similarity of two machines is estimated to be 1 in 3,000,000,000,000).

Feeling Light

Last comes forgery, and in this field free writing is one of the most skillful forms. It means the forger practices endlessly from the subject's handwritten models until it can be copied without an original. In time and place it can be successful, but it does not stand up when the expert examines the *corpus delicti* (which does not mean corpse but "the sum or aggregate of the ingredients which make a given fact a breach of given law").

Bank notes, postage stamps, and insurance stamps are fair game for forgers. But the false bank note is often marked by indifferent or incomplete work—these poor examples the forger usually passes in crowded stores or presses on busy cashiers.

Forgery on a massive scale is not always successful. During World War II the Hitler government produced numerous £5 bank notes as a weapon against Britain—hoping that the counterfeit money would cause chaos in businesses and banks.

The full technical resources of German experts were used, and with what result? Ultraviolet light showed that the ink was different; there was a fault visible to the naked eye just above the B in the *Bank of England* watermark; and the watermark also had three lines too many on one sample as well as two lines lacking in the second.

Finally, a forged note and a real one were given to an ordinary bank cashier, who was blindfolded. He indicated the forgery immediately—it did not "feel" right.

Conduct unbecoming

In love or war, what is right for one person seems wrong to another. A love relationship is fraught with taboos as well as accepted rules of conduct.

Love is about choices: choices about whom to love and when; about how to show love and respond to it; about which pleasures to seek and which obligations to fulfill. How to make the most of love while it lasts and what to do if it breaks down; how it affects your relationships with others, your acceptance of responsibilities and attitudes to social conventions, laws and regulations. And these choices involve your moral beliefs.

Morals reflect a person's conscious ideas about how people should act and think, emotional reactions that stem from past experiences, education and upbringing and the effects of interaction with other individuals and society at large. And behavior based on moral precepts implies that a person will plan his actions and take responsibility for their consequences. For some people, moral beliefs, although they may be shared with others, are treated as guidelines for the individual's own use; others see moral precepts as rules that should be universally applied to everyone.

Sexual morality is only one aspect of moral behavior. Love requires keeping promises, honesty, respect for others, and avoiding harmful conduct just as much as any other relationship or sphere of conduct. But in a sexual relationship love can involve decisions which are influenced by strong emotions. And love can affect the growth of a tie or hasten its destruction.

Love for some people overrides all other loyalties: whatever responsibilities they have—whether supporting a family, undertaking a contract, or playing a part in the community—these would be set aside if love happened along. For many more people a relationship founded on love represents the first and most important loyalty, which is nevertheless tempered by other responsibilities. After marriage, for example, a husband and wife may learn to back each other

Taking a chance on love, goes the song. And where love's concerned that's exactly what you're doing. Will he do her right? Will she do him wrong? Will they be happy-ever-after? For lovers, time alone will tell.

against criticism from parents whom they would once never have questioned, but not totally to disregard the wishes and happiness of other people. And still others may see a sexual relationship as subservient to some alternative aim, whether service to society, the pursuit of power or money, or the provision of an heir.

The Tie that Binds

And ideas about morality in love can reflect very different views about what love should be. For some people sex is irrelevant to the morality of a relationship: they would regard only something like the exploitation of one partner by the other as a matter for condemnation. Many believe that love and sex are intertwined, that where there is love sex may follow, but that sex solely as a pastime or a physical indulgence is to be avoided. Others suggest that the external recognition of a relation-

ship through a civil or religious marriage ceremony legitimizes sexual contact that could not otherwise be countenanced.

According to their view on the connection between sex, love and society, people see marriage itself as a widely differing kind of institution. And these different concepts of marriage can, in turn, affect people's attitudes towards sex. Accepting marriage as the divine recognition of an indissoluble bond may lead a person to reject as immoral sexual intercourse outside that bond. If on the other hand marriage is seen as an open and registered avowal of a couple's commitment to each other, they may not condemn sex outside marriage as such, but may forswear it as likely to reflect the breakdown of their relationship.

Where marriage becomes a contract recognizing the exchange of services and guaranteeing the security of any

Graham Percy

children or a pact agreeing to have a particular kind of emotional involvement with each other only, then sexual contacts with people outside the marriage may be a matter of pragmatic availability rather than morality. And people who believe the quality of the relationship is what counts may live together without marriage, or marry and divorce as the changing relationship demands.

Sex before marriage gives rise to equally differing views. Premarital sex may be seen as immoral in any context or as permissible within a loving relationship, especially one likely to lead to marriage. It is sometimes regarded as a period of adjustment and experiment that will allow a person to establish strong and rewarding relationships with others in later life. Obviously young people are most affected by these attitudes. Some refrain from sex until after marriage, others make love after they have been going steady or become engaged, some enter exploratory and extended relationships without intending marriage—though indeed they may—and a few indulge a taste for promiscuous adventure.

"My mother and I used to have long arguments about premarital sex," said Celia. "She would say it was completely wrong under any circumstances, that no one would respect a girl who gave way, and if she and my father could go through a three-year engagement without jumping the gun then anybody could. I'd scream that she was living in the past and that she made sex sound like something evil —but, curiously enough, talking with the girls at school I was the one who announced that I'd have sex only with someone I really loved and that he'd have to be ready to marry me.

Getting Together

"Then when I went to art school I met Peter. He was about three years older and due to graduate from another college that year. He already had fixed up a job in the city. We spent the winter wandering on his campus hand in hand and then in the spring he moved into an apartment. Rather than face a trek back to my apartment in the dark I took to staying over at his place—Peter slept on the couch in the main room and I used his bed. But emotionally we were getting closer and closer. Eventually I was the one who suggested we sleep together. We

Some families sunbathe as naked as nature intended, while others, voluminously wrapped in robes and moral certitude, prefer to boil with heat and indignation.

didn't make love that night—although we were so aware of each other we stayed awake until dawn—because we didn't want to take any risks about contraception. But it was worth waiting the few days to visit the advice center on the campus and to know that we both realized what we were doing.

"Later that month I moved in with Peter . . . we'd made that kind of commitment to each other—but we didn't actually tell my parents. The worst part for both of us was my fear of being found out. I'd go through deceptions like creeping back to my neighborhood to mail letters so it would carry the right postmarks. My mother sensed something was going on and for a while, whenever I saw her, she'd start talking about how I should save myself for marriage. But when she met Peter, you could almost see her falling for his charm.

"Both my parents have got to know him quite well now, and although they've never said anything—and certainly haven't said they approve—it's clear they've realized we're living together. My mother's taken up a new tack, too. Now she's concerned that I'll marry too soon, before I've finished art school. But there we're actually agreed. When Peter and I started making love I thought it was a step on the way to marriage. Now I've realized that's a decision we've still to take.''

Adultery gives rise to the same sort of moral opinions and options, sometimes complicated by its illegality under certain jurisdictions. Responsibility over arrangements for supporting dependants together with the use of contraception may, as they may with premarital sex, reduce the economic and pragmatic consequences of a liaison outside marriage to a minimum. For many people exercising prudence in this way is all that morality requires. Some might see adultery as unfortunate but nonetheless not affecting the central core of the marriage while others believe that adultery must mark a marriage's end. And those who understand love as a complete commitment to another person may see sexual intercourse with a third person as incompatible with continuing the relationship, whether marriage is concerned or not.

Moral Questions

Sex within marriage or within a relationship can raise moral questions specifically related to the kinds of activity involved. Some forms of sexual behavior, even between consenting husband and wife, are classed as illegal.

Alfred C. Kinsey suggested that if all laws about sexual behavior could be rigidly enforced then an extremely high proportion of the population would find itself in jail.

Some people may consider that the illegality of a particular caress makes it immoral, others that, since sexual intercourse is intended for procreation, they should not indulge in forms of sexual activity that cannot lead to fertilization. Still others accept variations on the sexual act as an enjoyable addition to a repertoire of love-making techniques, believing that only when the act is harmful or inflicted by one partner on the other without consent does it become immoral.

Public and private morality has always differed widely whatever the fashion in "deviant" sexuality. Thus homosexuality is currently considered revolting while Victorians abhorred the errant husband.

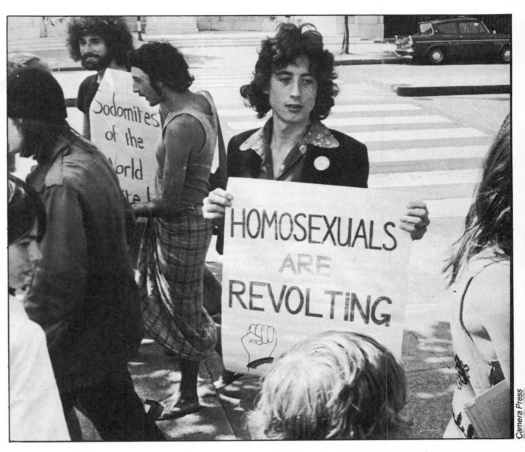

Contraception, too, can raise problems both inside and outside marriage. Opposing the use of contraceptives usually concerns the argument that the natural purpose of sexual intercourse is to produce children and that the expression of love and the experience of physical pleasure are tangential to this aim. For those who hold this view, contraceptive methods —whether mechanical devices or hormone-containing pills—are an offense against nature. Nevertheless, the Roman Catholic church accepts that a couple are free to express their mutual love and quieten their physical urges by having sexual intercourse at times when the woman is likely to be infertile and unlikely to conceive.

Spacing a Family

"Maria is Catholic," said James. "I'm not. But before we became engaged I spent several sessions talking with a priest at her church so that I could understand the commitments I'd be making in marrying her. I've agreed that our children will be raised as Catholics, for example.

"Planning our family was one of the areas that we went into fully. Maria and I want to establish ourselves before we have children. If Maria can work for three or four years we should have enough money to afford a house, and as long as my plans at work go smoothly I'll be able to support a family. The priest explained the church's position on contraception and helped me see how important it would be to Maria not to go against that teaching. But he also explained that the church does not stand against planning the spacing of a family and even suggested that we ask Maria's family doctor for advice.

"Both of us were virgins then, and we didn't make love together until our wedding night—we'd always been agreed about that. So her doctor gave us what virtually amounted to a short lecture on what love-making involved. Then he went on to explain that a woman produces an egg roughly halfway between two menstrual periods. By not making love for a few days on either side of that point we could put off having children until we were ready for them. He suggested to Maria that while we were still engaged she record her temperature every day and note when each of her periods began. Shortly after the egg is released, apparently, her temperature would rise slightly and stay like that until her next period. By checking what she'd recorded on a chart the doctor could advise us when making love would be least likely to lead to pregnancy and, if necessary, could prescribe drugs that would regularize her monthly cycle.

"So far this rhythm method, as he called it, has worked out fine. Of course, we'd be happy if a baby did come along, even though we're not looking for one yet, but we really want to go another year or two before starting a family."

On the other hand, people who accept contraception as part of love-making may consider immorality lies in *not* using methods to prevent another unwanted child from entering the world. The force of this belief can lead doctors and parents to provide contraceptive advice for teenagers who, while still under the legal age of consent, consider themselves mature enough to enter or prepare to enter a fully mature sexual relationship.

As an alternative, abortion carries, for many people, a heavier moral burden than contraception. Some do believe, however, that up to a certain stage of pregnancy abortion should be available as an adjunct to the provision of contraception. Although there is argument as to what the stage might be and as to whether a difference arises from the necessity for a full-scale operation later in this stage compared to the simpler treatment possible earlier—and although there is general agreement that effective contraception would have been preferable—abortion is seen as a better alternative than an unwanted pregnancy. Often such socially pragmatic attitudes are reflected in the different abortion laws of various countries.

Grounds for Abortion

Some people believe that only risk to the mental or physical health of the mother, or an inadequate environment for the care of the baby, gives cause for abortion. Others feel that the life of the mother must be weighed against the life of the fetus before abortion becomes allowable.

Part of the argument about abortion revolves around deciding at what point the fetus can be regarded as a human being. Many people in favor of allowing abortion consider the fetus becomes human only when capable of life outside the mother's womb, while those opposed suggest that the embryo is alive and capable of full human development from the moment of fertilization. This is the fine point that reconciles people to the idea of abortion when they are opposed to euthanasia, the easing into death of old or handicapped people who wish to give up the struggle to live.

For a sizable proportion of the population of western industrialized countries, questions of sexual morality refer not only to the conduct of relationships between one man and one woman but also to those between people of the same sex. Those homosexuals able to avoid legislative interference encounter much the same moral problems as heterosexuals in working out how to deal with situations such as initiating or ending a relationship. Many people believe that the sexual activities of consenting adults in private—whether homosexual or heterosexual—should not be exposed to moral censure by others. However, those who wish to label homosexuality as immoral suggest, for example, that private behavior may nonetheless affect the tenor of society as a whole and should therefore be open to moral comment.

Approaches to sexual morality, as to morality in general, take different forms. Some people find a source for moral rules in divine revelation; others look for guidance in the traditional beliefs of the society in which they live. Some people try to encapsulate their moral principles in a single overriding statement; others, at the other extreme, hope that their intuitive reactions to each situation will reveal the appropriate solution.

But confronting the problems of sexual involvement is ultimately a matter for each individual and should become more than just avoiding the prohibitions of the legal system and the strictures of moral belief. People have more to offer each other than being conventionally right and good—and love may be one of those offerings.

Just as love is about choices so too are morals. And what is moral for one individual is immoral for another. If each person could learn to respect the moral beliefs of other persons and perhaps come to some accommodation with them then this could be a happier world in which to live.

So too if communities learned to respect the beliefs or traditional values of other communities there might be less war and more of a chance for peace. But tolerance is a human quality that has improved little in the past few centuries. We have made some progress, but only with social reform.

Those who pay lip service to visions of idealized love know only too well from the depths of their own experience that fairy tales don't have such happy endings.

Carol Birch

Decline and fall

As a man grows older he will come to most things colder, deafer and blinder by and by.

Last scene of all,
That ends this strange
  eventful history,
Is second childishness and
  mere oblivion,
Sans teeth, sans eyes, sans
  taste, sans everything.

So Shakespeare described the last of man's seven ages, and while we may today accuse him of exaggeration—since many more people are living to a hale and hearty old age—it is nonethe-less true that many of our senses degenerate as we get older.

Nobody is really sure *why* we age: there is no apparent reason why body cells should not go on living indefinitely, provided they have sufficient oxygen, water and a few other simple nutrients contained in our food.

Yet body cells—notably those of the brain—do die and are not replaced. Body systems slow down and lose their strength and resilience. The arteries harden with deposits and become narrower, the muscles can no longer exert the forces they used to in youth, the bones become more brittle, and the joints are less able to bear the stresses on them.

With care, exercise and a sensible life-style, we can delay many of these processes and remain fit and active well into our eighties or nineties, but we are still unable to overcome the effects of age completely. Although modern medical science now ensures any individual a dramatically increased life expectancy over the last century or so, all it has done really is to guarantee more people a greater chance of attaining old age. Man's "natural span" is still little more than the biblical three score years and ten.

As one of Britain's leading gerontologists (those who make a study of the aging processes), Dr. Alex Comfort does not foresee any dramatic change in the length of life in the near future. He has written, "The best we can hope for from medicine and hygiene *alone* is that the average life span will increasingly become 75-80 years."

And despite the claims of many so-called rejuvenating drugs and preparations, he adds, "There is no graft, hormone or other preparation which is at present capable of producing more than a limited reversal of a very few senile changes in human beings."

Out of Sight

Of all the degenerative processes that occur—and many of them have begun on the day we are born—it is those of the senses which are most noticeable and tend to detract most from our full enjoyment of life. And of the senses, sight and hearing are undoubtedly the most vital, although our decreasing capacities of taste and smell do detract from life's full savor.

Often, sight problems are purely hereditary and can begin very early in life. Some people, for example, inherit an eyeball depth which is shorter than average. This means that the light rays all tend to focus behind the retina and the eye's lens has to be thickened even for distant objects. Such people are known as farsighted. Conversely, others quite naturally inherit eyes which are longer than average where the light tends to focus in front of the retina: such people are nearsighted. Many farsighted people overcome the extra focusing problems, but the nearsighted could only make distant objects sharp by making the eye's lens thinner, and this is impossible.

Vision problems are overcome by using artificial lenses in spectacles or, increasingly nowadays, contact lenses, small transparent disks which fit snugly over the cornea.

Any lenses simply bend light rays to ensure a sharp picture at the retina. For nearsighted people, concave lenses are used to shorten the focusing length. And for those who are so farsighted that the eye's own lens cannot compensate sufficiently, convex-lensed spectacles are provided for accurate focusing.

Our eyes grow with our bodies, so, because children's eyes are shorter, they tend to be farsighted. The growth is not complete until the child is between 14 and 18.

The children who are eventually to end up with eyes that are longer than average—that is, who become nearsighted—will go through three periods as their eyes grow: farsightedness, normal vision, and nearsightedness. This may mean that they will have to change their glasses regularly during their growing years.

Most people have a great deal of false information about vision. In truth, absolutely no harm can come to the vision by wearing the wrong spectacles, someone else's spectacles, or no spectacles at all. You cannot ruin your eyesight by reading in a dim light, or strain the eyes themselves by overuse (although you may strain the muscles that control their movement, which can lead to fatigue, irritation and headaches).

Throughout life the lens of the eye continues to grow, and as we get older it becomes thicker and less elastic. This is a completely natural process —just like graying hair—but it does mean that it becomes more difficult for the muscles around it to control its thickness and, therefore, focusing ability. Although this change is going on all the time, it usually does not really become noticeable until the late forties or early fifties. But at this time it can begin to make focusing for close objects more difficult, and spectacles may be needed for reading. The thickening and hardening process continues into the seventies and eighties, and it may mean that older people need to change their glasses for stronger ones every two or three years. But spectacles do not cause, or accelerate, the changes in the eye: these are natural and unaffected whether you wear spectacles or not.

Failing Vision

There are many myths about the eyes in middle—and old—age. An expert has written, "One tragedy that ophthalmologists and opticians often meet are the old people who, because they have something wrong with their vision, deliberately abstain from reading or watching television in the mistaken idea that they will harm their eyes.

"There are also those people who have only one working eye and try to spare it because they think it has to do twice the work. There is absolutely no basis for this belief. No healthy eye can be damaged by use and there is

hardly any condition or disease which can affect the eyes where continuing use of them can cause any further damage.

"We have only to think of the ears —another organ of special sense just as complicated and intricate as the eyes—and we know that nobody has ever suggested that they have stopped listening to this or that in the belief that this might save their hearing. The concept of eye strain is a widespread and largely erroneous myth."

As they get older some people may find they need help for both close and distant focusing. Often they will have two different pairs of glasses, but increasingly people are turning to spectacles which combine lenses for both these tasks. Called bifocals, the lower part of the lens is ground to provide sharp focusing for near objects while the upper part is used in focusing at a distance. They may take a little getting used to, but many people find them much more convenient than having to keep track of two pairs of glasses.

Cloudy Corneas

Contact lenses, too, have increased in popularity in recent years, particularly since the introduction of very soft transparent plastics used in lens manufacture. Many people do find them difficult and irritating to wear at first, but in most cases the eyes quickly get used to them. For those who are concerned about the appearance of spectacles—and particularly the girls who believe, like the American humorist Dorothy Parker, that "men don't make passes at girls who wear glasses" —contact lenses are the answer.

Another of the problems connected with the aging eye is cataract, a clouding over of all or part of the lens, which admits light to the retina. It may be due to a variety of factors, and it is so common that almost everyone has cataract to some degree.

As we get older, however, the cloudy areas tend to become more widespread, and in the elderly the changes may occur much more rapidly so that vision is seriously impaired. Happily, cataracts can be safely treated nowadays by a simple operation in which the clouded lens is merely removed. This straightforward procedure means that enough light is once again reaching the retina. Spectacles, or even contact lenses in some cases, are then used to help focusing.

Another problem which is commoner as we get older is diseases which cloud the cornea, the transparent coating of the eyeball. Again there

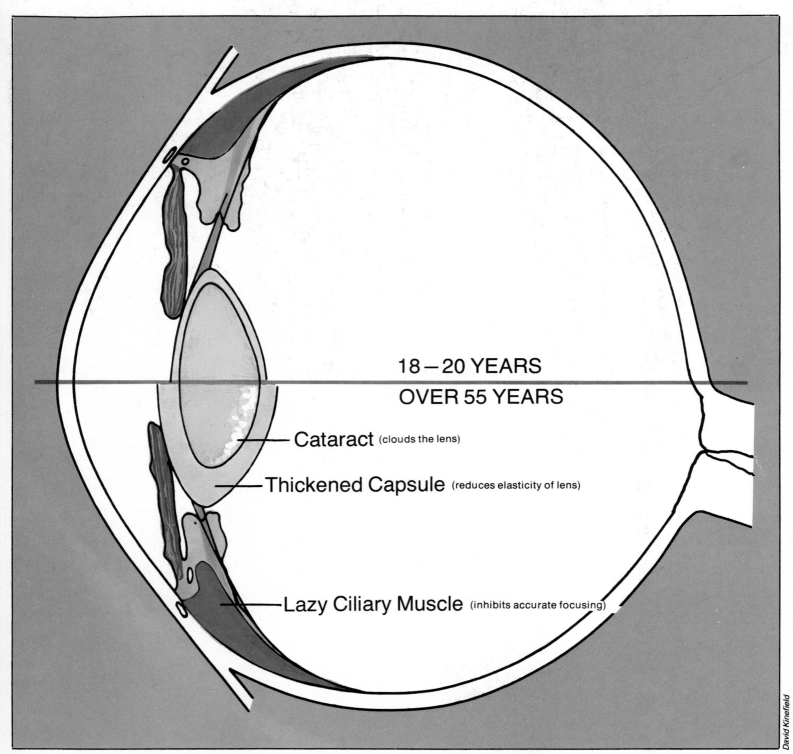

18 — 20 YEARS

OVER 55 YEARS

Cataract (clouds the lens)

Thickened Capsule (reduces elasticity of lens)

Lazy Ciliary Muscle (inhibits accurate focusing)

David Kinefield

may be a variety of causes. Today such problems may be overcome by a corneal graft, where the cloudy area is replaced by a clear section of cornea, either from the patient's other eye or from a donor. Hundreds of corneal grafts are now being successfully performed every year, although one of the big problems is that there are not enough donors to supply all the patients who might benefit.

Eye experts stress that there is really nothing specific you can do to preserve or enhance your vision. Their advice is to leave the eyes alone: if the

rest of you is healthy the eyes are usually well able to look after themselves. As you get older, however, they recommend regular checks—perhaps every year or two—even if nothing seems to be wrong.

Like the eyes, the ears really act as relay posts, translating outside events —in their case, sound waves—into a form of nervous signal that the brain can interpret. It is the brain itself which hears and understands by analyzing these signals.

As we age, the hearing process begins to work less efficiently, affect-

No one can prevent his sight from failing—yet how thin the line between youth's perfect vision and the obscurity which may creep up on us all with age!

ing the higher-frequency notes first. The mechanisms of decay start very early: very young children, for example, can hear the high-pitched cry of bats, but by the time they reach their late teens or early twenties it has become inaudible.

Much of the so-called deafness in old age involves the inability to hear

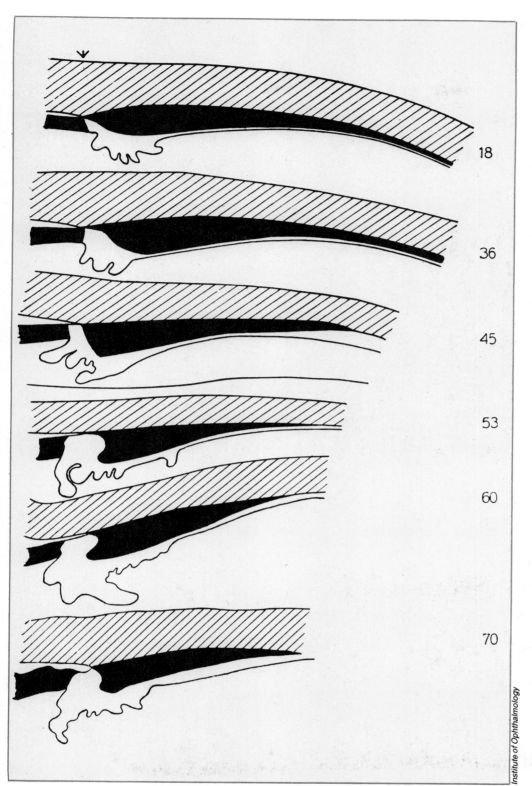

18

36

45

53

60

70

As this diagram shows, the shape of the eye's muscles changes so gradually from 18 to 80 that few people see what is happening before it's already too late.

the higher-pitched sounds. The difficulty is that in speech the consonants are pitched much higher than the vowels. If you cannot distinguish them, speech becomes unintelligible. Shouting at such old people does not help very much: they can hear the sound

well enough, they just cannot distinguish the consonants. Hearing aids can be helpful in these cases by picking out and amplifying sounds so that the higher frequencies can be heard.

Deafness is divided into two main types—*conductive* deafness and *perceptive* (or nerve) deafness. In conductive deafness something goes wrong with the passage of sound to the inner ear. It could be wax, inflammation, infection, or a variety of factors interfering with the free flow of

those vibrations. In many cases this kind of deafness can be prevented from becoming permanent by antibiotics or by an operation to remove any obstruction or repair a damaged eardrum. In some cases hearing aids may be needed to bolster the flagging transmission system by amplifying the sound waves traveling through it.

In perceptive deafness, the trouble lies within the organ of hearing itself or in the nervous pathways linking it with the brain. Several specific diseases can cause perceptive deafness, but it is also one of the consequences of aging—the system simply is not working as efficiently as it used to. It has to be admitted that nerve deafness is invariably permanent and that at the moment there is little that can be done medically or surgically to help it. Research is going on, however, into the possibility of implanting tiny electrodes into the cochlea to restore some of its lost function. But it is likely to be years before work results in generally available treatment.

For the present, hearing aids are often the answer, for by boosting the signals reaching the inner ear they give the flagging system more information on which to work.

Hearing Aids

It is vitally important that anyone who thinks he is becoming hard of hearing has his hearing checked by properly qualified people. Diagnosing precisely the hearing problem in each individual case is a skilled job, as is the proper tuning and fitting of a hearing aid best suited for the particular patient's need. Because there are some unscrupulous manufacturers around who make exaggerated claims for their appliances and charge a lot of money for them, you should always seek expert advice, ideally through your doctor in the first instance.

Although overuse of the eyes does not cause permanent damage, assaulting the ears for long periods by really loud noise can cause lasting harm. By and large, everyday noise does not seem to affect our long-term hearing, but we have created many industrial processes where noise reaches dangerous levels.

People who work in car factories, steel mills, bottling plants and the like may be subjected to noise levels of 90 to 100 decibels—that's like a noisy motorbike revving up a few yards away from your ear—every day of their working lives. Studies have shown that they are 14 times more likely to suffer from hearing loss, especially in the higher frequencies, at the end of

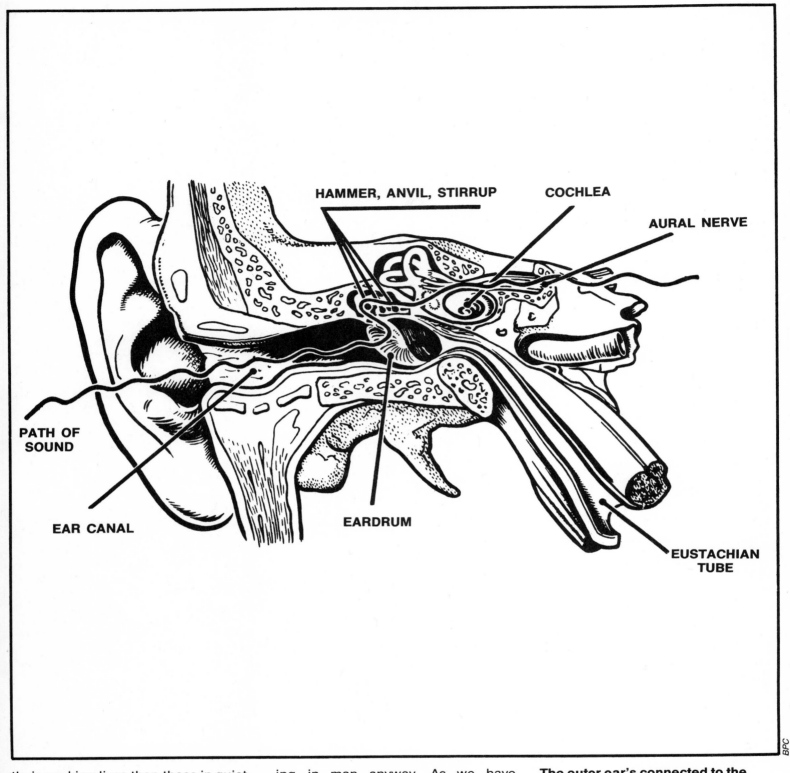

HAMMER, ANVIL, STIRRUP   **COCHLEA**

AURAL NERVE

**PATH OF
SOUND**

EAR CANAL

EARDRUM

**EUSTACHIAN
TUBE**

BPC

their working lives than those in quieter occupations. People in such jobs really should wear ear protectors.

As far as the other senses—taste, smell and touch—are concerned, man has not yet invented devices to bolster them in old age. It would be impossible in touch, since there are so many receptors scattered over the body. Taste and smell are not essential senses in the same way as sight and hearing, although they add much to the quality of life. But there is already evidence that both of them are declin-

ing in man anyway. As we have evolved we no longer need them for survival, and our sense of smell in particular is far less developed than that of most other mammals.

As more and more people live to a healthy old age, the problems of the degeneration of the senses will become more widespread. There is no way to stop the processes until we understand more about aging in general, and even then it is doubtful that there will be any effective remedial action. But at least the

The outer ear's connected to the middle ear, the middle ear's connected to the inner ear, then you "hear" the sound in your brain. In other words, sound passes along the ear canal, beats on the eardrum, vibrates the hammer, anvil and stirrup bones and is converted into nervous energy for the brain.

aids we have developed for the failing senses of sight and hearing enable millions to enjoy alert and communicative later years.

Child's play

United we stand—divided we fall. From childhood we depend upon groups for survival.

Human beings have always had a tendency to gather into groups. The composition of these groups, the reasons for their formation, the tasks they perform and their psychology are vital to us all, for we are the raw material out of which the group is made.

The one identifiable factor that has characterized all groups—from the most primitive to the most modern—is that they depend on cooperation from their members in order to survive.

The majority of groups to which we may belong in adult life resemble to some degree the patterns and functions of the family group. It is within the family, with its multiple types of relationship—husband-wife, mother-child, father-child, child-child—that we first learn the value of belonging to a group and take the first steps towards socialization, the process of learning to live with others.

The married couple conceive and the child is born into his family group, whether he likes it or not—there is no element of choice. Similarly he is a member of other so-called primary groups—a race, a nation, perhaps a religious group. Later the child will belong to a school and maybe a club. Increasingly there will be groups that he chooses himself, called secondary groups. In one family the father may be a Freemason, the mother belong to the Women's Voluntary Service, the daughter to a tennis club, one son to the Scouts and the other to the YMCA.

Personal identity is closely related to racial or national inheritance. Many social studies show that the individual's sense of personal identification with his national group is a major determinant of attitude, character and behavior. In the world outside the home other forms of groups reflect and enlarge the family-group pattern. The school, the university, the business firm, the church, local administration, political parties—all these groups function broadly on the principle of the extended family, each demanding a certain degree of loyalty and conformity while at the same time making allowances for individual needs, skills and expectations.

Children naturally come together at an early age to create some sort of social "pecking order."

The individual's choice of secondary groups reflects, for the most part, his personal interests, personality structure and immediate needs. He may choose to join a particular religious sect or a certain political party, not so much because it satisfies him intellectually but because it best serves his emotional needs. When a group gets together for a specific and rational purpose, the initial impulse and its original patterns can be seen most clearly. After that it may blur.

A Hive of Bees

Children's gangs are spontaneous groupings and have no such specialized motivation as do, say, the symphony orchestra or industrial monopoly or chess club, whose purposes are precisely defined. Children come together with an impulsiveness which is so much a part of their social natures that it is notoriously difficult to hold them together in any formal grouping before the age of about 14. Children do compete, but more to establish an internal hierarchy in their gangs—the "pecking order," as it is sometimes called—than to enjoy any formal competition. In the apparent teem and swarm of the school playground there is an internal order, understood by the children, which is as rigid as the order underlying the swarm of a hive of bees.

Membership of a secondary group, as of a primary, enables a person to identify with others who will provide him with continuing support and who will give him opportunities to establish himself as a significant member of the group and accord him his deserved status.

At times there may be a degree of friction between the allegiances demanded by the various groups to which one person belongs, reflecting conflicting feelings and attitudes within the person himself. In some countries, the loyalties and animosities created by secondary groups—those groups where an element of choice is possible—can cause

Spectrum

a particularly drastic division. Dangerous social situations easily develop, for example, where religious convictions run deep, as in India between Hindu and Moslem or in Northern Ireland between Roman Catholic and Protestant religionists.

An everyday example of this conflict of interest is found in the commonly experienced tension between the family and the adolescent peer group. In the course of the long process of establishing his own identity and increasing independence from the family group, the adolescent is likely to rebel against the attitudes, convictions and moral standards of his parents. He tends to reject wholesale everything they stand for. He is saved from a crushing sense of personal isolation if he can, for a period at least, belong to a group of people who are of his own age and who are also going through a similar stage of development. That way he won't feel so alone.

Human beings learn by imitation and the ability to follow example and instruction: their existence depends on this ability. They use imitation in learning how to talk and acquire the skills needed to perform the great number of apparently simple but necessary acts of life. The necessity for grouping and relationships may have arisen from this learning process, for the group passes on the body of experience necessary for survival.

The family provides three main advantages for the individual and, to a greater or lesser extent, this is true for all groups. Firstly, the family makes certain unspecific demands on each member to ensure that he contributes within his capabilities to the good of the group. He must learn to conform; it may limit his freedom but, at the same time, it is a necessary element in the process of social adjustment.

Secondly, the family group provides rewards and penalties in order that its essential unity may be preserved as long as may be necessary. Rewards may take the form of praise, approval, gratitude or appreciation. Penalties include blame, censorship, limitation of freedom, temporary exclusion from the group, and imposed guilt when other members are injured.

Finally, and most important, the family provides a particular type of secure framework for its members. This security is broadly based on mutual affection, mutual trust and shared aims. An individual is not alone; whatever happens to one member of the family is bound to affect all the other members. Within its framework, the individual has a place, a status of his own, and the other members provide support and encouragement. Within the family environment, too, the individual member is free to be himself, to express his thoughts, his doubts, fears, hopes and moods, without being afraid of too much harsh criticism. He is free to express his negative feelings of hate, resentment, dislike, and depression, knowing that the group will usually understand and tolerate the resulting tension, and will not cease to love him.

Social Aggression

Of course these are all theoretical ideals. Various critics point to the growing numbers of people in our society who have scarcely acquired the rudiments of a human or civilized culture—a growth in the incidence of what Patricia Morgan, a British sociologist, calls Feral Man. She points to the sharp increase in crime, violence, and aimless destruction of all kinds, with large proportionate increases as one goes down the age scale. She also looks in alarm at the volume of crime, often of a highly dangerous and serious nature, which is committed by those well under the age of criminal responsibility.

As she puts it, "Vandalism, once an uncommon occurrence, is now automatically accepted as an inevitable fact of the urban environment; even gross cases are hardly worth reporting. Actually, to use the expression 'crime' for much modern antisocial behavior is more than rather misleading, since it has no end beyond the most transitory titillation. The delinquent is frequently far too unsocialized to control his pursuit of instant excitement for rational gain." There is a high rate of maladjustment or emotional disturbance reported in school children, many of whom are excessively aggressive.

Not all these problems by any means are attributable to social deprivation in the sense of poverty. Delinquents, for

Spectrum

example, frequently come from families who by most standards are well housed, well fed, well dressed and physically healthy. What Patricia Morgan is fundamentally bringing into question is the psychological foundation of our Western theories of child rearing and child care. She questions the popular theory of the nuclear family and the need for an intimate relationship between child and mother as being the only healthy way to rear children. This is commonly seen as part of a wider ethos which attempts to explain goodness, maturity and responsibility in the individual wholly in terms of private and personal family relationships, leaving out the rational transmission of a social culture.

Frustrated Intellectuals

In place of this often faulty system, she pleads for an approach based less on the emotional ties of the nuclear family and more on a recognition of the part played by society at large. Far too often, our nuclear families are isolated, the parents young and inexperienced with no one to turn to for help, advice or encouragement.

She feels that the role of the school must be broadened, along with a general widening of the guardianship and upbringing of children. "There is a need for both creches and nursery schools to be created as an integral part of housing units. Ideally some of the staff should be well known and resident in the area. The emphasis must be on an opening up of the nuclear family, a sharing of parental functions by people who become involved with children not biologically theirs. There should always be people available in any area for advice and emergency child care. But what is crucial is that the deliberate professionalization of child care be avoided. To be shunned like the plague is an emphasis on qualifications and certificates, surrogates for degree courses, one year, two years, three years, filled with the speculations of frustrated intellectuals whose only idea of extending parental responsibility would involve extension of their own pseudoexpertise."

The Soviet Union has gone a long way towards providing alternative care to parents for the rearing of their young. For over half a century it has provided early group care of children on a broad-scale basis. Russia once had extensive residential facilities for the young, but more recently it has supported group day care for large numbers of infants and preschool children who live at home, together with a continuing program of residential care for children with special needs.

Good Social Traits

The clarity of goals in these group care settings is striking. The Soviet citizen and especially the staff of the preschool are well aware of an explicit set of values and desirable traits towards which optimal child development is thought to lead. This is in contrast with many other Western countries where neither such awareness nor such a consensus is found. The Soviet child teacher-cum-caretaker is oriented towards well defined cognitive and moral goals. Each game and activity is carefully designed to produce particular skills and to emphasize the collectivist values and character structure.

Another alternative society, as opposed to the nuclear family, has been provided by the Israeli kibbutz. The word *kibbutz* means "group" in Hebrew. The kibbutzim or communal settlements of Israel are agricultural communities which have been established at intervals during this century, mostly by groups of young immigrants from European countries. They are dedicated to certain values, in the words of the social scientist E. E. Irvine: ". . . laying the agricultural foundations of the Jewish National Home in Israel; the creation and maintenance in each kibbutz of a classless society, with equality of manual and intellectual workers, and of men and women; the creation and maintenance of an educated peasantry; the high estimation of manual work; and the subordination of the individual to the community."

Bruno Bettelheim, an authority on

Life is a long process of learning to fit happily into social groups. First, membership in a family (left) is necessary in most societies. Then you have to learn to live with others (right) in demanding situations.

children's emotional development, has written a book called *The Children of the Dream* in which he attempted to discover just how institutional child rearing affects the children themselves. He spent two months of intensive research at one kibbutz, visiting many others while interviewing a wide variety of people.

. The so-called children of the dream are the first Israeli generation to be born on kibbutzim. From four days after birth, they spend most of the day and all of the night with their age group, living not at home with their families but in separate children's houses, under the care of members of the kibbutz assigned to that task. Each child is in the care of a nurse or housemother, known in Hebrew as a *metapelet*. The metapelet of the infants' house is a specialist, and remains behind when the group of four to six infants moves from an infants' home to a preschool nursery.

During the first year of life, and particularly until the end of the nursing period, the mother participates a great deal in the care of the infant, though neither the mother nor the metapelet sleeps with the children. There is a rota of special night watch-women in the children's house. At age seven the youngsters move to a children's society (including school and home) and from the ages of 12 to 18 to the "youth community."

The founding of the kibbutzim and their ideals are in large part a reaction to ghetto existence in Europe. Bruno Bettelheim observes that all the satisfactions that in the ghetto had come from family ties, and many more, came to kibbutzniks from their peer group. Hence their greatest fear was that if men and women were to stop sharing the same life activities, if women were to turn again to a preoccupation with pregnancy and child care and the men to competing for a living, then the group would cease to meet their emotional needs.

The emancipation of the woman and complete equality of the sexes was one of the most important goals of the kibbutz from its inception. It was among the most passionate expressions of the revolt against bourgeois society. The socialist Jew could not accept the rejection of womanhood which is so much a part of Jewish religion. The essential female role in the ghetto was one in which the woman's entire life was swept up in nurturing and serving husband and children, and nothing else. This sort of ritual rejection of femininity by their parents and their own glorification of masculine pursuits meant that the first kibbutz generation viewed man's work as preferable to woman's.

Equal Care

But later the determination to free the woman from her traditional role became one of the sources of communal education. The communal nursery—it was thought—would open the road to real and not only formal equality.

When the break with the past came, it was complete. Bettelheim states, "To the founding woman, her mother's life seemed so overwhelming an example of giving to children, so much all of one piece, that she could not imagine herself identifying with part of it, and not others. These mothers of theirs, in their single-minded devotion to family and children, seemed most powerful figures to their daughters. To be free of such an image, one had to be free of it *in toto*. The daughter could not conceive in her unconscious of being able to take care of husband and children and still be an equal companion to men. She felt she could not do that much better than her mother. But she felt she could do things entirely differently."

Scientific Abstraction

It should not be forgotten that children in kibbutzim form strong emotional bonds with their parents and have a lot to do with them, although the daily contact is limited. The child is relating to more people during his formative years, and this has been thought by some theorists to be potentially damaging. Others disagree.

The eminent anthropologist Margaret Mead believes that "adjustment is most facilitated if the child is cared for by many warm, friendly people." The social scientist G. Lewin stated that "collective education has . . . proven that the existence of more than one image in infancy is not only not harmful for personality development but, on the contrary, may be a very important psychohygienic factor. Identification with the mother alone is a scientific abstraction."

Bettelheim, at the end of his investigations, concluded that while communal child rearing has its problems, these are outweighed by its advantages. The young kibbutzniks, while somewhat subdued in their affection for individuals and lacking in ambition (perhaps a commune value which is desired anyway), are more stable in many respects than conventionally brought-up children, far less prone to delinquency or neuroses. This conclusion is confirmed by many other studies.

Bettelheim sums up his experience by saying, "The kibbutz experience clearly demonstrated to me that children raised by educators in group homes can and do fare considerably better than many children raised by their mothers in poverty-stricken homes, and better than quite a few raised at home by their middle-class parents."

You learn to cooperate as well as compete by playing sports.

David Levin

Alter ego

Look into the mirror's golden eye, reflect, and perhaps you will see others as you see yourself.

Joy comes to life through love and friendship, through watching a family grow, through involvement with work and the community. Sex can be part of it, and so can the slow growth of mutual respect. Appreciating a fleeting contact with another person gives pleasure which shades into the comforting atmosphere that surrounds a group of people who have known and liked each other for some time or, at the other extreme, human pride in some achievement by strangers a continent away.

Empathy provides the key to finding joy through relationships with others. This sympathetic understanding of what they feel allows for the very real experience of knowing how to recognize and satisfy those needs. Getting inside someone else's skin opens the way for the most rewarding kind of personal contact. And at the same time it is a faculty that provides personal reassurance: anyone who feels able to understand the motives and aspirations of others and who is willing to help in their attainment must feel that others can reciprocate this kind of care.

Understanding starts with imagination, the sort of imagination that knows other people are both similar and different, ready to be reached and at the same time jealous of their own separate existence. Listening carefully to what someone else is saying, knowing what there is to know about the background, and judging how far he or she is presenting a one-sided view of a situation are all important—but imagination allows primarily for appreciating what all this means to the person involved. Empathy means more than thinking "How would I feel if that happened to me?" Its essence lies in thinking "How does the person that this is happening to feel?"

Overall similarities between people increase the possibility of this empathetic understanding. When the gulf between them is wider, the imaginative strain necessary to bridge it can be too great even for those aware that their own experiences offer only a very tentative guide to how others see life.

As Others See Us

Reading foreign news reports, for example, whether of disaster or high achievement, encapsulates all the difficulties of comprehending existence within a different political system, at a different economic level, and under different physical conditions. People from industrialized Western societies can attempt to understand the experiences of others who have lived in isolated peasant communities; some anthropologists have reached the point where they cease to study a tribe and instead become one of its members, continuing to live within the tribe instead of returning home. But just trying to picture physical and social life at the other end of a single town suggests some of the obstacles.

Empathy may well have serious limitations as a social force. When many people are unable or unwilling to explore other viewpoints, there is little chance that an intuitive appreciation of social needs will emerge in a public forum. But within the closer grouping of a circle of acquaintances, and particularly in the close involvement of love and marriage, empathy has a great part to play.

Two people who share many of the same experiences and who hope to achieve many of the same things together often find that they have taken up virtually the same attitudes towards these experiences. Just a short step from realizing that their attitudes are often the same takes them to knowing what the other's attitude will be and even to appreciating their feelings when, for some reason, their attitudes differ. And understanding each other's feelings in this way can help direct communication. Everything about their relationship—from decisions about buying new kitchen equipment to the greater enjoyment of love-making—benefits when they feel they can see into each other's mind.

"Our marriage almost went on the rocks, and only about four months after the wedding," said Greg. "Our sex life was on the verge of petering out. We'd started off badly because neither of us really knew what to do. I was embarrassed about sex—I'd never been out with any other girl but Rosie—and, looking back, I know she felt much the same.

"That might have been all right if we'd actually been able to talk to each other. But we weren't saying anything to each other in bed either. The days would go by as though nothing was the matter, we'd ask each other's opinion about things, go out together in the evening, hold hands until other people actually began making jokes about the lovebirds and then, at night, go to bed in the darkness and scrabble around in silence. Or rather I'd roll on top of Rosie and hope that tonight that wonderful thing would happen.

"Of course, we were just making each other more and more frenetic. Those nights when we did have sex Rosie would be left dissatisfied—I could feel it in the way she'd lie tensed up, careful not to touch me. I'd experience little more than physical relief, and sometimes not even that. We began talking about going on separate holidays, although without mentioning the real reason to each other—'It will give us time to breathe,' we said.

"Before that happened, however, I found myself in a long heart-to-heart with Wendy—she's married to Alan, who's been my best friend as long as I can remember. I happened to be over at their house—waiting for Alan to come home from the office—and, well, Wendy's one of those people who seems to persuade you to open up your innermost being. I told her what I'd been going through, and then her response floored me completely. 'Have you imagined what Rosie thinks of it all?' she asked.

Siding With Rosie

"I suppose I'd been expecting some expression of sympathy and that would be that. Getting it off my chest might help a little but that would be all. Instead of that, Wendy made me go step-by-step through my marriage looking at it from Rosie's point of view. What did I think her attitude towards sex was? Did she want to enjoy love-making? Did she think I was just some crude figure out for my own enjoyment? Did I think *she* would be able to talk to *me* if I never talked to her? How would I feel if I were Rosie, being made love to in that way.

"I'm not sure it's really possible for a man to get inside a woman's mind, but after the way Wendy spelled things out I made a real try with Rosie. Oddly enough, the first stage was easy—I told her what I was trying to do. But I left out the fact that I'd talked to Wendy about our difficulties. Once I'd started to realize that Rosie probably felt just as lost and embarrassed as I did, talking to her became much

easier, and she began to appreciate, too, that I was nervous and shy, not bored and demanding as she'd half begun to think.

"We've got a long way to go before we can pretend we're in the top league of lovers. But we've got a baseline to work from. Now when I caress Rosie I don't think, 'This must excite you'—it's too easy to treat someone almost like a machine or like an extension of yourself with no desires of her own. Now I try to feel it as though I am Rosie, and she tries to do the same for me. We're trying to make love both *to* and *for* each other."

Emotional Telepathy

Understanding of this sort, where both people concerned try to assess what really matters to the other by feeling it themselves, can spread throughout a relationship, bringing good effects of all kinds. To outsiders, it can seem almost like telepathy, as each seems to know what the other wants. But the real basis of empathy lies in very ordinary motives and character traits, coupled with the urge to want to know the other better.

Trust, honesty and loyalty, for example, are essential. For two partners to try to understand each other from within requires an openness towards each that cannot be ringed around with personal defenses. In learning about each other both have to reveal themselves—and their conceptions of the other person. Even within a marriage, husband and wife can be wary of swapping confidences, frightened, perhaps, of boring the other or, where parents often quarreled, of offering up ammunition for some future argument or dispute.

Seeing how another sees the world through a subtle form of imitation is much like an actor slipping into a characterization; his self-confidence is at stake as much when his attempts at understanding are rejected as when an audience fails to respond. Empathy between partners helps them confront the world together; where one withdraws from deeper personal contact the other's attempts at understanding result only in emotional floundering.

Benevolence and generosity are motives that help in establishing empathy. For some people altruism, offering aid without expectation of personal reward, becomes closely linked with the emotional contact of empathy. The deep inner realization of how difficult some other lives may be—whether a needful friend or acquaintance or a complete category of people such as the homeless

If you're locked in unhappy silence, compassionate fellow feeling may be the only key.

—leads the altruistic person to offer what help he can. In general, wanting to understand a partner more fully springs from wanting to establish a happier and more rewarding relationship, wanting to know what the partner's needs are, and looking for ways to satisfy them.

Awareness of what emotional experiences can mean is necessary, too. Empathy is an attempt to understand another's emotional world, but this can make sense only when the variety and significance of possible emotions are recognized. A person whose own emotional range is limited, and who shies away from discussion about emotions, does not have the background information to understand their significance in another person's life. And even a person who gives fuller expression to the emotions may be unused to identifying and analyzing the effect of these feelings.

Although empathy can play a part in every aspect of life, many people find

its greatest impact comes in making contact with someone unhappy or depressed, whether through an apparently unaccountable swing of mood, worries about a relationship or work, or a reaction to the death of a parent or friend. When happy, people are usually talkative and forthcoming, full of plans that often need only a little help to see them on their way, and someone able to enter this mood from within is likely to gain as much as he gives. Communication is often so easy that information is conveyed on many different levels, not merely by talking.

Lack of Communication

An unhappy person, however, is liable to become withdrawn and uncommunicative. Concentration on his own depression may put him in a state of self-absorption and self-pity that, while understandable, can discourage friendly overtures. Making allowances for behavior less sociable than usual offers a minimum of help, while sometimes insight into the person's state of mind suggests ways of giving more positive aid.

"Arnold's father has a very strong

personality," said Claire. "He doesn't really mean to, but he exudes this aura of solid success based on an implacable will. Arnold's always trying to live up to his father's image and I'm sure it leads to difficulties for him. About two months ago he applied for promotion in his job—and was turned down. He probably felt it more than most people because his father gives off this impression, and I don't know how true it really is, that his own life was one of unbroken upward progress.

"I was astonished to see just how badly Arnold took it. He came around here early one evening—David and I live in the next house to Arnold's family—to return some plates his mother had borrowed, and while I was making some coffee he virtually said that since he obviously couldn't be a success at his job he'd be better off throwing it up and spending the next few years on the beach. I'm no good at dealing with someone in that mood—I told him he'd already got far further in his career than anyone else of his age in the neighborhood—but David is. Because he's always making jokes and telling people to join in whatever's

going on he can seem as though he's only one step away from trying to screw a laugh out of a man facing a firing squad. But he is very aware of what people are feeling.

"That night he began talking to Arnold about his own start in business. David's just as successful as Arnold's father, but he doesn't give the same impression that it's due solely to moral virtue. In fact it took him about ten years to get going after he left school, and some of those years were pretty lean. Now normally when David talks about that period it's just for laughs—he can make every deal sound like an assault on the national debt. But that evening he just told Arnold straightforwardly about how he'd tried one thing and given it up, then another and another until finally some of them worked. I think it was the first time Arnold had realized that life doesn't need to be bulldozed into submission the way his father implied.

"Arnold's talking now of setting up a small firm of his own—says if it doesn't work out he'll always be able to go back to the kind of job he had before. I don't know how much influence David's little talk had on him, but I do know that it was exactly the right kind of approach to take at the time."

Some psychotherapists try to develop empathy from its status as an almost unconscious identification with someone else into a controllable therapeutic tool. Talent, goodwill and compassion, they believe, allow them to shorten the processes that lead to understanding their clients. The American psychoanalyst Theodor Reik suggests, in his book *Listening with the Third Ear*, that there should be four stages in establishing this close relationship with the client: identification, incorporation, reverberation and detachment. In the first three stages the therapist becomes able to understand the client's own view of his problems and in the last stage, detachment, is able to offer to his patient analysis based on distilled experience far wider than the client's own.

But empathy as a therapeutic technique—and as a possibility in everyday life—can have dangers. One is of becoming swamped by the imagined experiences of others. Living through another's emotions for a short period can help to provide a deeper bond between two people, but the excitement of indulging emotions at will can tempt a person into continuing this vicarious existence without noticing the effect on his own capacity for direct feeling.

Apparent insight into another's life can also produce an impression of power that gives a "right" to meddle without real basis. A sense of kinship that first allowed empathetic contact

Getting to know you—getting to know all about you—may take time, but by the look of this happy couple, being precisely one another's cup of tea is more than worth it.

with another may also seem to provide the justification for insisting that only those solutions imagined by outsiders have validity. And there is always a temptation to step across the bounds of privacy: two lovers may share virtually all their thoughts, but acquaintances must have areas of their lives that are kept from each other. The first step into another's emotional experience seems so rewarding that, without care, concern for his well-being turns to unmotivated prying.

Most important of all, however, is the distinction between sympathy and empathy. Sympathy provokes a person into offering help when help is needed, but it is based on an outsider's view of the situation. If that happened to me, thinks the sympathizer, I would welcome this kind of approach. But sympathy relies on similarity between the two people involved, and where there is a difference in character or cultural background the kind of help offered may be unsuitable. Empathy accepts that people are both similar and different and tries to make the promptings of sympathy exactly relevant.

Honor and obey

Whether your friendly neighborhood cop has a swinish look depends on your attitude to authority.

"Is this your car, sir?" asks the traffic cop.

"Yes, but . . ." we reply either humbly or defiantly. "Then move it," comes the perfunctory command. And we comply with the request or incur the consequences: a fine or the inconvenience and expense of having the car towed away and bailing it out of the police pound. The confrontation with the traffic cop is an everyday situation where a member of the public finds himself in conflict with authority. But what is authority, who has it, how does he come by it, and why are we obliged to defer to it?

On the face of it, the authority of the traffic cop has many facets. We may think there is something awe-inspiring about his uniform or compelling about his tone of voice, or it may be his physical size or the mysterious personal charisma he radiates which makes us recognize his superiority in this situation and approach him with diffidence. More likely it is because punitive powers are at his disposal if we refuse to cooperate. These may contribute to his authority, but they are not its essence. We comply because we accept that he is the instrument of some higher command.

If we were to search back along the chain of command to find the source of the traffic cop's authority, the quest would not end with the chief of police, the chief justice, the chief of the armed forces, or the head of state. Indeed, few of these exalted figures are legitimately immune from the authority of the traffic cop in matters of parking. The search would end where it began—with us.

We tend to regard authority as an imposition amounting to infringement of personal liberty and to associate it exclusively with the interfering people who enforce it. But authority itself is completely impersonal. There comes a time in our expedition along the chain of command when the last in line will point to a written law, a contract, an office or rank, a custom or a tradition, or even present some reasonable and logical argument and say, "This is where *my* authority comes from." Such authority remains operative whoever enforces it and, indeed,

Rosamunde Fearn

whether or not it is enforced at all. But it is only effective insofar as we agree to be bound by it.

Surveying the contemporary social scene, we see evidence that people are becoming less and less inclined to be so bound and that authority is losing its grip. Soaring crime rates and increasingly prevalent incidents of violence, delinquency, truancy, terrorism, anarchy and so on suggest that any ethereal or impersonal concept of authority is not particularly functional. Authority has to be enforced.

Meanwhile, the means the authorities use to stave off the rising tide of opposition and the excessive and corrupt practices those who supposedly have right on their side are increasingly being found to employ are gradually eroding public respect for authority. In the light of these trends which cast doubt on the validity of authority as it is at present exercised, it is suggested that the very principles on which societies are based are in need or urgent revision.

The Common Good

All political systems—to a greater or lesser extent—hinge on the idea that the common good is achieved by placing certain restrictions on personal freedoms, but only such freedoms as are incompatible with the rights and liberties of others. That man is naturally self-interested, grasping, and never-mindful of the interests of others is probably nearer the mark than the belief that he is a naturally social and considerate creature. It is at the point where individual interests, acts, or aspirations are in conflict that the intervention of some impartial arbitrator—loosely termed "the authorities"—becomes essential to order and the maintenance of a workable social equilibrium.

The authorities—government, administration, and forces of law and order—provide us with protection, services, and other advantages in exchange for our pledge not to infringe the rights and freedoms of others, and we agree to their having powers to ensure that we and our compatriots all keep our side of the bargain. When we clash with authority, it is not the authorities themselves we have challenged but the freedoms of others whom they represent. This is as it should be, but, of course, this elementary notion of a social contract is capable of a variety of interpretations and distortions.

The difference between political and social systems depends largely on whether they regard the first precept of the common good as being the will of the state or the collective wills of individuals. As we understand it, legitimate authority—which is embodied in constitutions, laws, political institutions, social mores evolved from experience, custom, tradition, and history—depends on our sanction, the consent of the majority as expressed through democratic processes.

We allow others to wield authority over us principally because it is convenient for us to do so. At this point we hear a chorus of protest. By what twist of logic can it be considered convenient to be harassed and moved on by traffic cops? It is only convenient in the sense of being the better of two evils. The person who says, "I have never given my consent to a traffic cop moving my car; if I had anything to do with it, there would be no such occupation," has not seriously considered the alternative.

Certainly the means by which the traffic cop comes by his powers are so remote that the objector might have reason to feel that he has not been personally consulted in the matter. But if he were to withhold his consent for even this one situation, it would take only a few uninhibited motorists to park in his front garden, across his garage doors or driveway, or in the middle of the street obstructing the free flow of traffic and blocking access to shops and offices to make him see his error and change his mind.

Faced with this alternative he would pray for the existence of some officer empowered to get traffic out of his way, but the cop must inevitably also have powers to tell him to get out of other people's way, which we estimate on balance to be a small price to pay. His prayer for order was answered by vision of forethought, and traffic cops emerged on the scene long before this unmanageable chaos arose, in the certainty that we would all submit to their authority rather than become embroiled in the shambles we would be reduced to if man's innate selfishness and lack of consideration were given free rein.

Organized Chaos

But even so, we have to settle for a bit of both. The chaos that arises in spite of the presence of officials to sort it all out looks to an outsider more like the failure of the authorities to cope rather than the upshot of our inalienable belief that authority should be as unobtrusive as possible. However, it is an unfortunate fact of social life that the more chaos there is resulting from the clashes of individual interests, the more the authorities are obliged to intervene.

This is as true of servicemen, customs officials, judges and so on as it is for traffic cops. They seem to impose limitations on our activities, yet for our own good. It is for our convenience that they establish the social conditions in which we can be free. But their usefulness does not end there.

One of the elements of a social contract is a certain amount of subcontracting. In any society there is far more work to be done, far more duties to be discharged and roles to be played than can possibly be achieved by any one person acting on his own behalf. Maintaining law and order is technically the civic duty of every individual citizen, so that in submitting to the authority of the policeman or judge we are doing no more than fulfilling our personal responsibility, but by remote control. We have delegated our duties to the authorities and their functionaries. By giving them powers to operate in their respective areas, we do not renounce freedom but gain it, since they lift some of our most irksome duties from our shoulders, releasing us to get on with what we want to do.

The tendency towards specialization in modern society, while allowing the individual to develop and perfect his abilities in his own field, precludes the possibility of his developing in other directions. Every man cannot be his own policeman, judge, or tax assessor, simply because he does not have the necessary training to equip him for these jobs. These are other ingredients of legitimate authority.

Chain of Command

Thus, if we go to the doctor and have no knowledge of medicine ourselves, we are obliged to accept the doctor's orders without a murmur. He speaks with the authority of his profession, from his specialized and superior knowledge which is supported by his qualifications. We place ourselves entirely in his hands and consent to his authority in the absence of legitimate reasons for not doing so. We have delegated all our own responsibilities in matters of health to him, just as we have subcontracted our own duties in other areas of jurisdiction to people more expert than ourselves, from the highest public administrator to the lowliest petty official.

In a highly stratified social system, we tend to think of society as a pyramid in which power and authority reside at the apex and are whittled down as we move towards its base. This is not so, nor is it particularly true that authority is somehow evenly distributed right through the pyramid. Rather, society is made up of a complex network of power structures and hierarchies which exist side by side. So although we would tend to place a high-ranking army officer in the upper echelons of the pyramid, when he has

Camera Press

to go into the hospital for an operation he is ranked with the humblest recruit in matters of medicine and finds himself reluctantly having to accept the authority which prevails in his new situation, obliging him to take orders from young doctors, nurses, and even hospital porters.

Our attitude to authority depends largely on our position in the chain of command and on whether we are accustomed to giving orders or taking them. But whatever our position, one thing is certain—we always have been and always will be subjected to some form of authority. Our first encounter with it occurs in infancy. The baby's acceptance of his parents' authority is in his own best interests and is necessary to his survival. In fact it is the basic fact of survival which underlies all authority. Without some form of supervision and control inhibiting basic instincts, life would not be possible, let alone worth living.

It is in an attempt to prolong his life that the child, the most vulnerable member of any community, comes to terms with the fact that mother knows best and that father has his best interests at heart even though he demands unpleasant tasks and imposes irritating restrictions. Thereafter the child comes into contact with other agents of authority—elders, betters, school-

teachers, policemen. His regard for them and respect for their authority is based largely on the observation that they can do things more competently than he can, although sometimes it is fear of punishment, reproach, or humiliation which motivates him to meet the demands they make of him.

Child psychologists say that a child both needs and likes to look up to some form of authority, since it gives him the security of knowing where he stands, but he will continually be putting the validity of that authority to the test. The desire for the sense of security which a rightful, just, and effective system of authority provides does not desert him in later life, nor does the tendency to do anything he thinks he can get away with.

Rotten Apples

It is at this early stage in life that our attitude to authority is formed. The person who grows up having no respect for authority has probably had one or other of two early experiences of it. One possibility is that he has been regimented, inhibited and victimized by, say, tyrannical parents and so comes to regard all authority as unjust and contemptible, going through life getting his own back. Alternatively, the guidance for which he searched may not have been forth-

Riot police in Paris 1968 found their uniforms a useful target for militant student abuse.

coming; his parents may have been lax, indecisive, neglectful, and permissive, in which case he will regard all subsequent forms of authority as weak and not binding on him, disregarding any kind of outside control of his behavior. Both attitudes are antisocial and can lead to the courthouse.

So although authority in general terms seems to work, this is just one of the reasons why it does not in all circumstances hold good. Why do we not live in a just, equitable, harmonious society, which our system of government based on common consent purports to create? There will always be segments of a society which refuse to be bound by the majority will. There will always be controlling elites capable of overruling the public will, there will always be circumstances in which two or more agents of legitimate authority will come into conflict and make contradictory demands, and there will always be institutions or individual officials who overstep the boundaries of their rightful jurisdiction or prove themselves susceptible to grotesque abuses of power.

In many people's experience, these distortions of our high-minded social

Popperfoto

identity cards, badges, and uniforms come to his assistance. Uniforms are the most convincing manifestations of power. They are principally a means of identification, but this does not explain the many strange attitudes and phobias we have about them.

Some people tend to cower at the sight of uniforms and if their experience is that those who wear them are hostile—giving orders, invading privacy, asking impertinent questions, hectoring or arresting them—then this is an understandable reaction. But if their experience is that uniformed people give answers, information and assistance and if their clothes enable the citizen to pick a station porter or a road patrolman out of a crowd, then uniforms evince respect and even affection. The train ticket collector's apparel saves him the bother of explaining his rights and duties to every passenger on a train and warns the free rider to expect trouble.

A uniform also has a variety of effects on the wearer and tends to reinforce his attitude to his own authority. The official who likes to throw his weight around finds the uniform a valuable part of his armory, which gives the public cause to associate uniforms with officiousness, intimidation, aggression. In this case the uniform gives its inhabitant the feeling of power which he might lack. Others may like uniforms because they appeal to their vanity and make them feel smarter and more dignified, a credit, they feel, to the institution they represent.

Uniform Response

But a uniform is not intended to be an extension of the ego of the person inside it. The person who feels ill at ease in a uniform because it smothers his own personality and individuality is nearer to having the uniform in its proper perspective. Its very purpose is to do just that; a contretemps with a cop is "a brush with the law," not an encounter with an individual policeman who has a wife and children at home and likes a drink as well as the next man, factors which we are honorbound not to exploit. If uniforms tend to aggrandize a person, it could be said that it is to compensate for the fact that he is only human underneath, to confirm him in his devotion to duty, and to remind the beholder that although he may be taller than the policeman he is not above the law.

It is difficult to decide whether obedience to authority is a natural instinct or the product of social conditioning in societies which need

contract are the rule rather than the exception, and it is no wonder that authority has a bad name. While it is duty-bound to keep society and its members in order, we are beholden to keep authority in its place.

We tend to regard authority with some suspicion. It is difficult for the errant citizen when the forces of law and order loom large over him to evoke some philosophical concept of the justice of it all sufficiently overpowering to dispel his feelings of exasperation and impatience.

When it comes down to brass tacks —for instance, the traffic cop situation—the confrontation is between two ordinary citizens. If they

When the finger of suspicion is on the end of the long arm of the law, the request to move along has a convincing ring to it.

were to meet on entirely equal terms the situation could easily develop to the motorist's advantage if he had superior powers of persuasion, so it is necessary to bolster the traffic cop's authority in some way.

One obvious way is to empower the official to mete out punishment. But this power has to be instantly recognized and accepted if it is to elicit cooperation and obedience. The official's authority has to be symbolized in some way, and this is where

Ron Haywood

The driver may have a traffic cop on his back. But the traffic cop has a sergeant, who has a chief of police, who has a magistrate, who owes his position of authority to the man in the street—and that includes the man driving along it.

increasing doses of policing, bureaucracy, and impersonal administration to maintain some semblance of order and harmony. But either way it places authority in a much stronger position than we might imagine and raises the possibility that all kinds of injustices and indignities will be committed in its name. Where authority overplays its hand, those who challenge it will justify their actions by pointing to a "higher authority"—concepts of human rights and liberty—which they feel, rightly or wrongly, have been abused or distorted.

The breakdown of law and order which the prophets of doom bemoan is due to the increasing incompatability of so many individual, community, and national interests and the failure of authority to reconcile them. It is difficult for those in power to make concessions to one group without damaging the interests of another. This makes any exercise of authority or interpretation of justice a very delicate and unenviable operation. It also makes law enforcement, which appears to militate against minority interests and wills, potentially explosive. Although the total system of authority may be motivated by the common good, it invariably has some disreputably rough edges.

Community spirit

These days it's not just crabbed age and youth that cannot live together.

The second half of the twentieth century has been an era of unprecedented social change, on a scale and with a rapidity that is painful for many people. The high rate of divorce, the prevalence of violence, the massive dependence on tranquilizers and alcohol, and the increasing use of soft and hard drugs are witness to the loneliness, frustration, boredom and despair which prevail in our so-called age of anxiety.

There are signs that Western society—and especially American society, which usually anticipates the future of other Western countries—is experimenting with new values and different life-styles. And as is usually the way, the young are giving a lead. Many are looking for alternative ways of living in groups which are sometimes bound together by religious faith, sometimes by a shared political ideology, sometimes by a predilection for drugs, but often for other reasons, especially economic ones.

New Groups for Old

Many reject conventional family life and are grouping together in "new families" in communes where they explore other ways of living and experiment with a variety of personal and group relationships. A survey by the Institute of Life Insurance Research Services — "Alternatives" — indicates that over a third of a sample of 14-to-24-year-olds thought that communes would become a natural alternative to traditional family life.

Of course, there is very little new to living, and over the centuries countless people have opted out of conventional society for one reason or another. Religious life has called many different kinds of monastic groups into existence, and there have been many idealistic, secular attempts to build a utopian society or community. Aldous Huxley gives an inspiring description of one such attempt in his 1962 novel *Island*. Another novelist, D. H. Lawrence, sought in vain to found a new kind of community, a way of life which would embody his theories and ideals about human nature.

Nations, too, like China and Israel, have attempted to encapsulate politi-cal and familial ideals of collective responsibility and sharing, in communes or kibbutzim. The flourishing and spreading of communes and other new types of social networks in the United States and Europe has been haphazard but dramatic.

Three Wishes

Communal organizations focus on three components: family, cooperation and the use of space. Taking the family first of all, it seems that the ideology of the group as a whole has a crucial influence on it. First and foremost, there must be a stable system of sexual norms within the family if the commune is to survive. Historically, any violation of this condition eventually leads to failure. According to American sociologist George Hillery—in his paper "Families, Communes and Communities," read in 1971 at Mississippi State University—there seems to be no middle ground: either the commune has families or they have to be totally excluded. And if they *are* excluded sexual relationships are either prohibited or surrounded by restrictions and sanctions.

A commune called H.I.P., founded in 1969 in an urban setting and made up of 27 college students and one child, had only one rule: "to have no rules." Sexual regulations were relatively absent, and the commune failed. On the other hand, Oneida, a "one family" group, of 253 individuals practicing a system of group marriage, lasted from 1844 to 1880. All adults were potential spouses, all children were potential siblings. In this commune there was no promiscuity; there was a well-developed system of norms; arrangements for sexual relations were made through a third party; relationships could be refused; incest was not permitted; members were not allowed to develop a relationship of "exclusive love"; and only certain persons were allowed to have children.

Oneida, devoted to individual perfection and communal good, found it necessary to control its sexual norms. To be without any restriction—and this is the age-old dilemma about freedom—is to be in a state of chaos.

Humans find a life without norms difficult or impossible to bear. Communes like the Hutterites, a rural group of Anabaptist religious affiliation, have very stable familial systems. The Shakers, another rural community, officially rule out sexual relations altogether, preferring to recruit new members to keep the group alive.

Mutual aid and cooperation are an integral part of communes. Among the Hutterites and the Shakers, in kibbutzim, and at Oneida—full communes in the sense that most activities take place inside them—a person's job and contribution to the group are determined essentially by the community. On the other hand, in partial communes—where members usually sleep and eat within the commune but spend a significant time outside—the definition of cooperative obligations is less formal or contractual.

In Lisa Place—a largely Mennonite religious urban commune of 92 persons (families, single adults and children)—the communard turned his earnings over to a central treasurer who allocated a cash allowance to individuals or families, based on their circumstances. The central treasury paid for houses, fire insurance, automobile costs, medical and educational costs and so on. Here the mechanisms for cooperation were highly contractual but the purpose was close to mutual aid.

Spaced Out

The way space is used in a commune is an important factor, often prompting the careful control of sexual relations. Martin Houses—which are Lutheran and, more generally, Protestant communes set up for Christian witness and "to experience community"—are made up of college students. They are probably able to exist as they do, according to George Hillery, because the sexes are segregated at certain times and also because members are frequently away from the community. Caphas, a rural commune of 25 Protestants (families, single adults and children) living close together, has two strict rules: no drugs, and people who are not married cannot sleep together.

Camera Press

It may be hip to take up communal life, but an equal share in musty rooms and dirty sheets is somewhat less than fair.

Even in the secular communes studied by psychiatrist Ross Speck, where extramarital freedom in sex was acceptable, the relationships were long-term and monogamous, with some of the quality of a trial marriage. Speck came across only one promiscuous girl who slept with any available man in the group; the men, in spite of occasional talk of playing around, were also monogamous. The family feeling is obviously a force to reckon with: one communard suggested that "every commune breaks up in the bedroom or the kitchen." There are, of course, polygamous family communes—the notorious Charles Manson's "family" was one—and occasional polyandrous setups with several men and one girl.

Some present-day communes have received a great deal of publicity, largely because they have been associated with wild sex and drug orgies. This is the image in the public mind, the popular stereotype. While the experimentation with and use of drugs has been an important theme in producing a subculture of the young, it is certainly not the only one.

In the United States and also in Western Europe, the drug phenomenon has escalated into a very worrying and newsworthy issue. It has been estimated that perhaps 50 percent of American youth of 14 years or over have at least experimented with psychedelic drugs. In places all over

the country pop music festivals have acted as a catalyst for political discussion among youths who came together to discuss the Vietnam war and draft dodging, to experiment with new ways of experiencing life and self-fulfillment, to make love and to freak out with music, drugs, and the euphoria of togetherness. But as Victor Gioscia observes, in his article "Acidoxy vs. Orthodoxy" in the *American Journal of Orthopsychiatry* (1969), the youth-drug subculture has invented a whole series of social institutions that parallel and mirror institutions of the larger society.

Noble Savages

The use of psychedelic drugs—to quote Ross Speck in *The New Families*—"was given great impetus by mass media coverage. . . . It spread by word of mouth like a religious movement. The drug phenomenon launched a romantic idealistic movement among youth, a wish for a return to the primitive, a Rousseauistic 'back to nature' movement, a questioning of ethics, morals, and values. Though the hippie movement was largely confined originally to New York's East Village and San Francisco's Haight-Ashbury, by virtue of the mass media, the love-ins and be-ins rapidly traveled back and forth across the country, infusing youth with their philosophy of love, peace, brotherhood, antiwar, do your own thing, racial equality, civil rights, and so on." Since 1965, when the communes in the United States were around 100, the figure has climbed to well over 3,000 in the 1970s.

Many themes seem to run together

in these new group life-styles; there is an association between youth, drug usage, sensitivity encounter groups, rock music, radical politics, existential philosophy, a preoccupation with mystical and oriental religions, an interest in astrology, and an atmosphere of protest and revolution. The "rejection of society" theme, although important, is less common than the mundane and practical reason of economics. Some also join out of a desire for personal growth, believing that cooperation in work and welfare of the group will be to the general advantage. Some communards are dedicated mystics, some are deeply religious, others atheists. Some are celibate, some believers in free love. Some are conservatives, others radicals and revolutionaries. There is no *one* stereotyped member.

Most communes have between 5 and 15 members, though there are some of over 1,000 members. They can be found in towns, in the country, and in the desert. Each social network has some overlapping membership with others, and a peripheral network of people who occasionally visit a particular commune. In a group of 10, this peripheral social network might involve 75 to 100 people. As many as 40 guests might visit within 24 hours: communal life tends to override the conventions of time so that some people in a communal house may be sleeping while others are eating, and yet others are playing games or entertaining. Usually it is only the evening meal that has any degree of predictability and even then not everyone bothers to attend. The pace of life is relaxed and somewhat disorganized.

Let us look at one commune housed in a dilapidated old building in one of America's major cities. The leader is Max, a 22-year-old university graduate of striking appearance with long red hair and red beard. He graduated in sociology and economics by dint of a clever reproduction of his lecturers' style of thinking and expression rather than meticulous academic application. As he likes to tell his friends, he conned them by playing the system and learning the jargon. Max has tried both hard and soft drugs but now only uses psychedelic ones and then only on rare occasions. He earns occasional sums of money as a jazz musician playing gigs where he can get them. He relies on his girlfriend Martha's steadier income as a writer for the underground newspapers.

Max also occasionally gets sums of money and food parcels from his parents who are well-to-do people from the Midwest. Although he has rejected his parents' values and beliefs, he occasionally phones to maintain contact with them and actually went back home for a brief period when his father was ill. His father visited the commune on one memorable occasion and, although sickened by the squalor and what he felt to be the aimlessness and immorality of his son's existence, he felt a sneaking (and unwelcome) admiration for his son's nerve in "doing his own thing" before he settled down. (This last bit of the equation was the father's wish-fulfillment rather than any stated plan of the young man.) Although not a political activist, Max regularly attends protests and sit-ins and strongly supported civil rights and antiwar issues in which his woman is interested.

Martha comes from a broken home: her parents divorced and her mother took up with a man whom Martha could not get along with. She dropped out of high school early and ran away from home at 16. It was at this time that she met Max, who was at college. Max became interested in her skills at expressing ideas and her ability at putting them down on paper. She had already begun to write pamphlets, and Max encouraged her to study writing and journalism. They became more involved with the drug scene and after staying in various communes started up their own in the old house which belonged to the parents of a friend. Martha and Max have one room out of the six in the house.

Their furnishings are sparse and have an oriental flavoring. The main item is a mattress on the floor. A battered chest of drawers contains a few clothes and on top of it are their books. The walls are extensively decorated with posters and pictures cut out of magazines and newspapers. One wall is a mural painted by an artist occupant of the house and depicts a drug-induced fantasy. The faces of the other members of the commune are attached to strange animal bodies and all are floating in a multicolored, swirling mist. Max and Martha are very proud of this mural and it is the only section of the room that they keep meticulously clean.

The artist, Mark, is a tall, thin 25-year-old from California, reserved to the point of muteness. He dropped out of art school because of a psychotic illness, but after prolonged treatment he is now beginning to do commissions for a commercial artist, though now spending more and more time on his own work. Mark is too inward-looking to be interested in women,

and he spends many long hours meditating on his own and apparently needs no company. Yet there are rare occasions when he emerges from his self-imposed isolation and then he seeks out Max and the others and talks volubly about art and about Van Gogh, his hero, before suddenly and without warning clamming up and disappearing back to his room and his life as a recluse.

Apparent Paradox

In another of the rooms live Phyllis and Marianne, lesbians who live a life of relatively quiet domesticity in this unconventional surrounding. Phyllis has a job in the respectable world outside. In a sense she lives a schizophrenic existence, being a competent and apparently middle-class secretary to a corporation executive by day, then returning to the commune at night. She adopts many of the patterns of behavior which are the norm in this communal setting, but she is the only member of the commune who does not use drugs. She has tried to dissuade Marianne from using them and only succeeded when Marianne became pregnant by an itinerant communard. Between them they had decided that, as a steady couple who had been together for several years, they would like a child of their own. For this reason Marianne accepted a liaison with a man who stayed temporarily in the commune. Her wish to become pregnant was fulfilled, and she and Phyllis are now bringing up a little girl together.

The remaining rooms are taken up by students living as couples, who spend most of their time outside the commune at college. Most have been able to organize their timetable so that they can concentrate their work into two or three days of intensive effort. One of the girls is pregnant and is expecting her child in a month. She is now beginning to talk about marriage to her partner, to the amusement of the others in the commune.

In a typical day at the commune, Max and Martha arise after 11:00 a.m. and come down barefoot for breakfast. Martha is a macrobiotic specialist and bakes whole-grain breads in a small electric oven. There is a pot of brown rice on the stove at all times. She gets a few bits and pieces ready and most of the others in the commune (except Mark) come down in dribs and drabs with their own plates and help themselves. The only person who gets up at a regular time is Phyllis, who has to leave for work.

On the days that there is a lecture or

laboratory class, the college students leave the house, but by and large there is always a group lounging around, doing odd jobs or entertaining themselves in the hours around midday and the early afternoon. Inevitably people begin to visit the pad during the afternoon and those who stayed the night before are leaving to go home.

As there are several amateur musicians and one professional in the house, there is always music either homemade or blaring forth from hi-fi sets in the different rooms. There is usually a group in the communal living room in the late afternoon, especially if someone has arrived with a supply of grass. Joints are passed around for the first smoke of the day. There is sporadic conversation and the occasional game of Monopoly. Sometimes these games go on into the early hours of the morning, esoteric games which the makers of Monopoly would not recognize.

A Little Night Meal

The night meal is a movable feast, and its quality depends on how much money there is in the house. If Phyllis has just been paid, it might be a real feast with Chinese food brought in. More often than not it is hamburgers or peanut butter sandwiches or crackers and cheese.

Most nights there is a party, with some heavy pot smoking while the lights are turned down low and the stereo turned up high with rock music. Four of the college students might enjoy a somewhat more sober game of bridge, and Phyllis and Marianne are usually the first to go to bed.

Despite the large number of communes, many individual members remain in them for relatively short periods, the average time being one year. Some theorists maintain that this might be due to the transitional stage of life through which many members are passing.

But as well as these temporary expedient reasons for joining, communal life is a genuine alternative, for many serious-minded adults of political, religious or other ideological persuasions, to the rat race they perceive our society to be. And in accepting people like Phyllis and Marianne, communes provide a stable way of life for those who might not have a place in conventional society.

Finally, the comradeship and the sharing of resources offer a warm, friendly and economically sensible existence to many people who would otherwise find life cold and inhospitable and threatening.

2836

Man and superman

Will *Homo sapiens* justify his name and generate a wise new world?

One of the facts science has taught us is that the planet we live on will not provide our home forever. Within four billion years it will be uninhabitable.

It has already been here for 4,500 million years, but for the first 2,000 million of those years it supported no life and it was another 2,000 million before life properly took hold.

Man himself really is a newcomer in evolutionary terms: the first recognizable ape-man groups appeared a mere 20 million years ago, and it was not until some 5 million years ago that our first really human relatives began to appear. In those last few seconds of evolutionary time man has confirmed his mastery over all other species and has given himself power—through tools, machines, and electronic gadgetry—over many natural forces, including gravity.

Quo Vadis?

But where does man stand now? How will he develop and evolve? Will he continue to dominate his planet—and beyond—in the years to come? Or will he blow himself up in an act of mass suicide?

We can only, of course, offer the most tentative answers to those questions, for man's future depends on a bewildering variety of complex, interrelated factors—some biological, some social, some economic. If we are to try to look at all into the future we must make some optimistic assumptions. First, political: we must hope that the different colors, races, nations, political persuasions, and religions will ultimately learn to live together and not unleash on one another the terrible weapons we have now developed.

Secondly, economic and social: we must hope not only that we can organize our agricultural capacities so that no one in the world will starve (and this is technically possible) but that we can learn to use the earth's natural resources with extreme care, for they too are finite. We must also find ways of developing alternative sources of power—perhaps directly from the sun itself—and of ensuring that our population does not become more than the planet can bear.

But assuming—and it is a very big assumption—that we can do all that, what will be man's physical and mental development?

There is no denying that children today are growing taller and stronger than their parents and grandparents. This, however, is due primarily to social factors, such as better feeding and housing, rather than to an evolutionary process. Over the millenia we can see that we have developed a much more upright stance than our apelike ancestors. We have become less hairy, our jawlines have generally receded and our foreheads expanded. Such evolutionary developments are by no means complete. Our backs, for example, are still badly adapted for walking on our two hind legs instead of all fours, and that is why back trouble is so common a complaint. Our teeth, too, tend to be too big or too many for our receding jaws and if uncorrected they often grow crooked and splayed.

As far as our looks are concerned, there is some evidence to suggest that faces in general are getting less rugged: cheekbones as well as jawlines seem to be softening. Ultimately, we may have little more than large, domed matchheads, with next to no striking features. Such developments are still a long way off.

It is, of course, man's brain which sets him apart from the other animals. But it is not sheer size that counts: elephants and sperm whales, for example, have bigger brains than men, and some monkeys have brains which are $2\frac{1}{2}$ times as heavy as ours in proportion to their body weight.

Instead, our superiority lies in the growth of our forebrain or cerebrum, which has now expanded to occupy all but a sixth of the total brain volume. The most important part of the cerebrum is its outer covering of gray cells called the cortex (from the Latin for cloak), for it is here that the most complex thought processes take place. Although the cortex is only about an eighth of an inch thick, it has so many convolutions and folds in it that its surface area is some 400 square inches. That *is* proportionately larger than any other animal, and it is

this which gives man his superior mental capacity and intellect.

We have already seen how late in evolutionary time man came on the scene. In fact, it is only in the last 100,000 years or so that he has really become intellectually communicative. And modern science, which has given us such amazing powers, really began only about 400 years ago. Within such a comparatively short time it has transformed daily life and our understanding of ourselves and our universe.

Some of the most fundamental discoveries—those in nuclear physics—have come within the last 40 years and given us both the frightening power of atomic bombs and the capability of unlocking the enormous energies within atoms for peaceful purposes. But the most significant scientific revelations, with the most awesome consequences for man's development, are being made at this very moment in molecular biology.

Medical and biological science began with concepts about the whole body; later it concentrated on specific organs. By the eighteenth century pioneer investigators were beginning to look through the microscope at the tissue of which organs were comprised and to see how changes in it could influence health or disease.

Inside the Cell

Later scientists began to look at the cells which made up the tissue and today we are inside the very cell itself, not only gaining a fundamental understanding of the workings of its constituent parts but also just beginning to unravel some of the complex biochemical processes by which the whole system works.

In particular, we are just beginning to develop the capacity for genetic engineering—altering or replacing genes, the units of heredity which pass on characteristics from one generation to the next. Admittedly we are able at present to do this only in the crudest way, on very simple germlike organisms. But it cannot be long before our capability is refined and extended. In 1964 one of the world's leading molecular biologists, Professor Joshua Lederberg, wrote, "The

UK Atomic Energy Authority

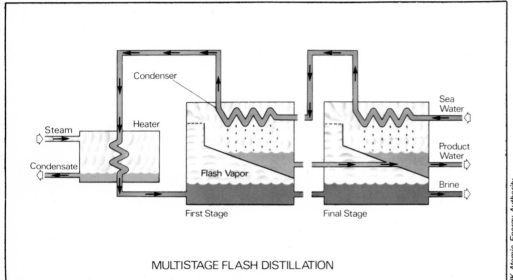

Condenser

Heater

Steam

Condensate

Flash Vapor.

First Stage

Sea Water

Product Water

Brine

Final Stage

MULTISTAGE FLASH DISTILLATION

UK Atomic Energy Authority

Man controls his environment with a multistage flash distillation desalinator (MSF) in Jersey, U.K. (top). A diagram shows the first two stages in the MSF process (above). Incoming seawater feed is preheated in condensers, further heated by steam, then distilled "in a flash" of evaporation.

sudden successes of biology, brought about by the systematic confluence with the physical sciences, now demand an understanding of the nature and destiny of man that must be the principal intellectual task of the brave new world."

Professor Lederberg emphasized the need to plan our society to meet the staggering possibilities being opened up in biology. The changes are coming very rapidly: Professor Lederberg's articles, entitled "A Crisis in Evolution," was among a collection of essays by eminent scientists, *The World in 1984.*

Among the great ethical problems being thrown up by medical and biological advance, Professor Lederberg mentioned the successful transplantation of vital organs—heart, liver, and kidneys. He said, "The technical barriers will be overcome long before we can reach a moral consensus on the organization of the market for allocation of precious parts."

Research is likely to bring also "a sudden increase in the expectation of life . . . Whatever our humanitarian predilections, discrepancies in the availability of these resources must widen."

Even more disturbing is the possibility of "the modification of the developing human brain through treatment of the fetus or infant." Professor Lederberg has warned that we can expect such modifications to be "constructively applied" to normal children—a chilling thought.

And just as radically disturbing is the possibility of reproduction by transplanting the nucleus of one living cell (containing all the genetic mastercodes and blueprints for development) into another from which the nucleus has been removed. In this way we could create a group of organisms all biologically identical. If and when such techniques become applicable to man it could be possible to produce groups of identical people, of a specially selected type to carry out specific tasks. We might require a group of especially muscular men for manual work, or brainy ones to act as a team on a research project, or aggressive ones to act as soldiers.

Using such techniques, the sex of every baby could be predetermined, hereditary abnormalities could be abolished, and we could accelerate the advance of human evolution by picking for reproduction only the best genetic types. But who is going to decide what is "best"?

Professor Lederberg observed, "I will be accused of demonic advocacy for discussing such matters and not pretending they are infinitely far off. But they are inseparable from the advance of medicine, especially as we turn our attention to such urgent challenges as mental retardation, the degeneration of aging, and mental illness. The scientific community has little special qualification to impose institutional remedies or moral criteria for the problems of human opportunity."

He added, "A deeper understanding of our present knowledge of human biology must be part of the insight of literary, political, social, economic and moral teaching; it is far too important to be left only to the biologists."

Those, then, are some of the moral and social problems biology has already created or will create within a generation or two. Our current social organization and way of thought seem inadequate to deal effectively with such complex issues. Is there any room for the individual in this kind of world? Does democracy make sense if we can physically manipulate brains and minds? These are the questions our children and our children's children will have to face up to.

Or will they? Could it actually be *we* who tackle the problems in 100 years time? One of the great unsolved mysteries of life is why people age and die. All our medical effort has achieved so far is to stop people from dying young by eliminating or controlling killer infectious diseases which a few decades ago wiped out millions before they reached maturity. Of course we still have to contend with the diseases of middle and old age, like heart disease and cancer, but more and more people are reaching the biblical age of three score years and ten. Indeed this is now the life expectancy for babies born in most developed countries.

Age Before Duty?

But why do body cells age and die? Why, given the right nutrients, do they not go on reproducing themselves forever? There are many theories on the processes of aging and it looks as if it will be many years before we really begin to unlock the mystery. Already, however, there are drugs which seem to be able to extend the lives of experimental animals. One of Britain's leading researchers in the subject, Dr. Alex Comfort, believes that, if enough money was put into research, similar drugs for humans could be found in five or ten years. With such drugs we could probably extend active life for between twenty and thirty years.

But think of the consequences: the population of the world would rise even more sharply than it is at present, and it would become top-heavy, with too few workers supporting too many pensioners. Unless, of course, we extended working life as well. Incidentally, few insurance companies or pension funds seem at the moment to be prepared for a major breakthrough in overcoming aging and postponing death. Since they are going to have to keep paying out year after year, it is about time they did. And it is about time, too, that the rest of us considered the implications of adding even another ten years to people's lives.

Although it appears we may be able to modify ourselves in the future, whether we will be able to exercise similar control over nature, over our environment, is another matter. Certainly we should be able to do so in the long term, but there is little possibility of, say, any really effective weather control within the next century simply because the forces involved are so vast and things like rainfall depend on so many complex interlocking factors. Nonetheless, advances such as satellites are beginning to give us a truly global picture of weather and a clearer understanding of the enormous system of forces at work. Within two centuries, weather modification should be possible. We will then have to decide what we want—sun all day and rain only at night, perhaps.

Transport should become even faster—and increasingly unnecessary as communications become so sophisticated that anyone anywhere in the world can talk to and see anyone else. Already organizations are beginning to abandon international meetings for closed-circuit television links.

On the energy front, it is obvious that we will eventually have to abandon fossil fuels and turn to either unlocking the gigantic forces trapped within atoms (by nuclear fission and nuclear fusion) or by directly harnessing the sun's power. Solar cells, which convert photons (packets of light energy) into electricity, have already been developed, although they are not very efficient and are at present very costly.

As far as food is concerned, we can expect to eat more and more vegetable protein; the soya bean, for example, is already playing a significant role even in Western diets. And we will be manufacturing protein direct from waste material, from vegetable matter like grass and leaves, and from hydrocarbons like methane and oil.

The most important feature of all in man's future development, however, will be what happens to, and how he uses, his brain. There is no reason to suppose that man's brain is not continuing to evolve, although it must be pointed out that evolution is a very slow process, to be measured in thousands, if not millions, of years, rather than in centuries.

Leap in the Dark

Our science has made great leaps in recent years, but we still have only the vaguest glimmerings of how many nerve cells there are in the human cortex. Some researchers put the figure at some ten thousand million, but others say there may be a hundred times as many as that.

What we do know is that the brain's hundreds of millions of specialized nerve cells are interconnected in highly complex nervous pathways, and we have actually traced some of the simpler pathways. We also know which areas of the brain are responsible for some functions, such as analysis of sight and hearing and control of the limbs. But we are still very much in the dark about the higher thought processes, what determines intelligence and how memory works.

Nonetheless there are signs that eventually we may crack the brain's codes. There is increasing evidence that a chemical called RNA (ribonucleic acid) has a vital part to play in the brain's storage of information. Because the nervous pathways are not straightforward electrical circuits, one brain cell communicates with another not by direct electrical connection but by releasing a chemical transmitter substance into the gap between them. Now when nerve cells are stimulated more RNA is used up than when they are not. And if the production of RNA is blocked, learning becomes impossible. This has led scientists to believe that the transmitter substances use RNA to build chemical storage banks within brain cells.

Subliminal Image

A fuller understanding of the mechanisms of memory and intelligence open up the way for manipulating the processes. Eventually we may, using chemical means, improve beyond all recognition everybody's capacity for storing and retrieving information. If we could all store more knowledge, we ought to be able to make more informed, rational and intelligent decisions.

The frightening aspect of all this is the perversion of the brain by psychological manipulation. We have all heard about brainwashing, but already the techniques of advertising have been used to create artificial demands in the mind. Politicians use similar techniques to sell themselves and their political ideals. Now that telecommunications have made the world a global village, such techniques could easily be extended to influence millions of people, probably without their knowledge.

The techniques of subliminal advertising—where an image is flashed onto a TV or cinema screen for such a short time that it is not consciously noticed but subconsciously registered—have been banned. But they do show what power over man's minds the unscrupulous could achieve.

More than ever before, the scientific advances of the next few decades —and the ensuing centuries—will carry with them enormous potential for evil as well as for good, and they will create enormous ethical problems.

The organization of our society is still based on concepts evolved long before the scientific era. We are going to have to take a long, hard look at those concepts if we are successfully to overcome the problems of man's future development.

Future shock

Our future is child of our past. But unless we take control it may grow up a monster, to destroy us all.

"Future Shock" was an expression coined by the writer Alvin Toffler in 1965 to describe the confusion and disorientation experienced by individuals and societies unable to cope with the stresses resulting from change. It is a process we can predict for our own society as technological change proceeds apace, and one which we can observe at work in others.

A large proportion of the human race is currently subjected to future shock: in Africa, as old tribal distinctions are broken down in favor of a Westernized culture; and in many immigrant communities, precipitated into a world which no longer accepts or tolerates the customs and ways of life in their native lands.

Social Disruption

It is a situation we in the West have already experienced. Over the past 300 years or so, industrialization has disrupted our traditional societies, breaking down the predominantly agricultural way of life formerly universal over Europe and North America. Historical studies in Britain show the misery and upheaval this inevitable process created in the agricultural communities which had remained largely unaltered for centuries.

Families who had lived in one village all their lives were suddenly uprooted and transferred to an urban environment. Those who remained in the villages often literally starved, because the traditional agricultural economy was destroyed by the introduction of mechanized farming. Those who moved to the cities often tried to return to their villages after finding that work was not available; they, too, sometimes starved, because their village way of life was no longer viable.

The same pattern can be seen repeated down the years to the present day. Warfare and plague in the Middle Ages was followed by social disruption. The cream of Europe's manhood went to fight in the Crusades—a pointless waste of life, from which many eminent families never recovered. The same stresses led to wholesale mental disorder: wandering flagellants beat themselves in public and religious pilgrims danced hysterically to the point of total prostration and even death.

These were all symptoms of the inability of ordinary people to adapt to radically changed circumstances.

Some examples are better known as culture shock, the results of being suddenly precipitated into an unfamiliar society. This was the result when Chinese laborers were brought over to work in the California Gold Rush and when Irish immigrants arrived in the United States after the great potato famine. It has occurred countless times in the United States where, apart from the Indians, immigrants and their descendants make up the population.

It is evident even now, in the camps set up to house Vietnamese refugees. These people remain in a pitiable state, neither Oriental nor Western. Because of their long association with colonial powers and military allies, they are no longer socially or culturally acceptable to most of their countrymen or neighboring states. Equally, many Americans are reluctant to accept their partially Americanized recent allies as permanent members of their nation. The Vietnamese will probably remain refugees, just as the Palestinian Arabs have remained victims of Isaeli-Arab conflict.

But how relevant are these dramatic examples to the probable future shock which the bulk of mankind will experience? In his book *Future Shock*, Alvin Toffler points out that it is already a cliche to say that we are now living through a "second industrial revolution." A great acceleration in changes to our way of life began with the turn of the nineteenth century. Since then, the technological advances and social disruption of two world wars have provided added impetus to an abrupt alteration in life-styles. In the 1970s, the rate of real innovation began to falter, influenced by world food and energy crises. But the rate of change is not diminished; if anything, change has accelerated.

Future shock, for our generation and the next, may well involve adaptation to simpler life-styles. Recent generations have become adapted to the technological world and instant pre-packaged foods, but if the gloomy predictions of the energy pundits and ecologists are proved true, the next few generations may have to revert to

an energy-sparing, self-sufficient society, reminiscent of that of a century ago. This is an extremely pessimistic view, but clearly we shall have to make dramatic changes.

Most Western society is built upon the availability of cheap, rapid transport. Highways, railways, airports, and docks are the arteries of our civilization. But when the predicted exhaustion of oil reserves occurs in a few decades, this huge economic structure may well become redundant. Unless unforeseen alternative forms of transport can be found, it will be necessary for communities to be largely self-sufficient and to rely on slower forms of transport like canals to carry goods long distances.

Technological Revolution

In *The Foreseeable Future*, the British Nobel Prizewinner Sir George Thomson suggests that the closest parallel to the future shock we are now experiencing is not the industrial revolution but the "invention of agriculture in the Neolithic Age." The American writer John Diebold comments that "the effects of the technological revolution we are now living through will be deeper than any social change we have experienced before." And the economist Kenneth Boulding observes that "the world of today . . . is as different from the world in which I was born as that world was from Julius Caesar's. I was born in the middle of history, to date, roughly. Almost as much has happened since I was born as happened before."

This last statement is not as improbable as it may appear. The human race as we know it has existed for about 50,000 years—approximately 800 lifetimes. But at least 650 of these lifetimes we spent as cavedwellers. Only for the last 70 lifetimes have we been able to pass down accurate information to our successors, since the invention of writing. And nearly all the manufactured goods we use today were invented or perfected in the present, 800th lifetime. How ironic if all this is to be thrown away, should mankind be forced back into a pre-industrial society as a result of dwindling resources and increasing populations. The future shock we have so

2841

Archigram/Ron Herron

The sprawl of the future "world city" will not stop at the ocean shore. With land at a premium, cities will be built to walk on water.

far experienced is nothing compared with that which may be in store.

The most helpless victims of future shock are those whose habit patterns are rigidly fixed. Elderly citizens become steadily more separated from the mainstream of society as the rate of change increases. Their grasp of reality is based upon the time when they reached maturity, and this inevitably seems more appealing than the confusing modern world. Reminiscing provides a link with the period when life was understandable and stable but also serves to further alienate them from the new generations.

The elderly are obviously resistant to change, but in our rapidly moving society many are "elderly" at 30. Even young parents bemoan the fads and fashions of their children. They deplore their morals, involvement in protest movements, drug abuse, outrageous clothes, bad manners, and so on. The 30-year-olds are as much the victims of future shock as are their own parents. But while today's young adults readily recognize the difficulties experienced by the elderly in keeping up with our changing society, they will be reluctant to admit to the same problems themselves.

C. P. Snow, the eminent British novelist and scientist, has commented on this problem. "Until this century," he notes, "the rate of change in society was so slow, that it would pass unnoticed in one person's lifetime. That is no longer so. The rate of

change has increased so much that our imagination can't keep up."

Changes in our way of life are nowhere more marked than in the increasing spread of urbanization. Little over a century ago, there were only 4 cities in the world with populations exceeding a million. By 1900 there were 19; by 1960 this figure had increased to 141. At the present rate of increase in city dwelling, we will have to build new cities at an unprecedented rate, to the point where much of the available land surface becomes a vast, unmanageable urban sprawl—the "world city."

Going Underground

Our ability to construct and maintain such a monster depends on the continuing availability of food and raw materials to support increasing world populations, and farsighted planners are now considering new ways to make the best use of our current resources. Underground cities are already a possibility, and plans have been prepared for vast ocean cities on partly submerged rafts. Both projects would minimize the exploitation of land surface, which could then be used for agriculture. But could we adapt to life in such surroundings?

The United Nations has considered several plans for the world city, assuming a population of up to 19,000 million. Such an urban sprawl would either cover almost completely the coastlines in temperate and equatorial regions or circle the earth with floating rafts. The social stresses resulting from life in such conditions have not been considered in detail, and accurate predictions are clearly imposs-

ible. But already the effects of increasing urbanization are clear.

In most large cities, and especially in specially constructed new towns, the quality of life has proved deficient. Increasing crime rates, vandalism, and rioting are closely associated with high-density housing. Even worse, the inhabitants of high-rise apartment buildings have a vastly increased rate of mental disorder. Living as they do in total social isolation within a high-density population leads to a feeling of alienation from society. "So many people, yet we never see them." Many do not know their own neighbors.

Even more distressing is the effect of such housing schemes on children, who are much more vulnerable. Lack of play areas and social contacts are producing a generation of victims of future shock, disturbing omens for a world metropolis.

Our problem seems to stem from a sort of primal schizophrenia. The unique human mind has an inbuilt drive leading us in a neverending search for knowledge, but as we acquire new knowledge, this inevitably brings with it a change in our way of life, a change which we are ill-equipped to deal with. Civilization is in many respects a denial of our basic instincts.

Mankind developed as a species best fitted for living in small communities of, largely, family groups, up to a couple of hundred strong. We are mentally equipped to thrive in such circumstances, living in small agricultural or hunting communities, as man throughout the world has done for thousands of years. In the few such groups still untouched by civilization, populations remain stable, and mental illness and sicknesses resulting from stress are almost unknown. Primitive man is as well adapted to his environment as any other form of wildlife.

But once primitive man is civilized, he has to take the disadvantages of change along with the benefits. Physical illnesses may be cured by modern medical treatment; fewer babies die at birth; people survive longer. But at the same time the social structure of the tribe breaks down. Populations that have not fluctuated for thousands of years, being closely tied to the availability of food in the area, suddenly lose their stability as they experience cultural shock. A tribe may plummet to total extinction, as happened to the Carib Indians and the Patagonians, or may gradually decline to a level where it is no longer viable, as is now happening to South American Indians in the path of the Pan-American Highway being cut through the forests. Or

Camera Press

The dome of the Palace of Congress in Brasilia—the showcase capital of Brazil. But though this beautiful city is an architect's dream, few go to live there, preferring the urban chaos of Rio de Janeiro or Sao Paulo.

populations may explode to unmanageable levels, as the built-in regulators of food supply, infant mortality, and premature death are eliminated—the process we are now seeing in much of Asia and Africa.

While many of the diseases which scourge primitive people are controlled by civilization, they are more than compensated for by an increase in the maladies of civilization. Cancers, heart disease, and mental disorder all become more common as population density increases. How common might they become if mankind is shoehorned into a vast world city? Without room for the individual or scope for the development of small social communities within the city, there seems little hope for happiness and contentment with life.

Our way of life in a more mechanized society is impossible to predict, but we may learn something by comparing our present way of life

with that of a century ago. In the nineteenth century and before, people were born, lived and died in one place. Villagers regarded people from neighboring communities as foreigners. In the United States, with a sparse population in relation to a huge land area, such insular feelings were understandable. Indeed, they had a positive function in that they helped to develop a strong community spirit. But even in Britain, where only a couple of miles may separate villages, the same spirit developed. There were, and are, minor dialect differences even between neighboring communities.

Driving to Distraction

Rapid transport changed all this. It made possible the dormitory suburbs which surround all major cities. It also encouraged the penetration of sophisticated former city dwellers into rural communities, as they were able to live in the country and commute to the cities to work. In many areas, this takeover of rural communities is causing social stress and protest by the dispossessed agricultural workers, now unable to afford house prices in a suddenly desirable area.

American culture probably suffers

most from future shock. Californians frequently commute hundreds of miles each day, and traveling has become a way of life. Futurologist Buckminster Fuller has calculated that, in 1914, the average American traveled about 1,640 miles each year, and of this 1,300 miles were covered on foot. This amounts to 88,560 miles in a lifetime. Today, in contrast, the average American *drives* more than 10,000 miles each year, and as he lives longer probably travels more than 3 million miles in his lifetime.

In any Westernized nation, travel is the most obvious feature. Even those outside conventional society—the nomadic hippie subculture—rely on travel, covering most of the United States, Europe, and the Near East, and regularly journeying as far as Nepal in their wanderings.

Among householders, traveling is also becoming a matter of course. In a single year (March 1967 to March 1968) 36½ million Americans changed their residences, making Americans probably the most mobile people in the world. This is reflected in the high proportion of rented, as opposed to owner-occupied, property in the United States.

The same pattern is repeated in Europe. Huge numbers of Turks, Yugoslavs, Algerians, and Spaniards form armies of migratory workers in Europe's industrial centers. And there is the notorious "brain drain" of European scientists, engineers, and doctors to the United States and Canada. Few migrants seem to make a permanent home in their country of work, being prepared to move on when better prospects present themselves. So the stream of aerospace engineers that in past years headed for NASA and its associated industrial plants is now diverging to related industries around the world.

Significantly, the degree of mental illness, suicide, and disturbance is extremely high among migrant workers and their families, from whatever social grouping they come. Coalworkers, technicians, scientists, or physicians—all migrant workers are subjected to greater pressure and stress than the native population. When recession strikes, they are the first to be laid off; in times of hardship, they are singled out as scapegoats. Their children suffer through language difficulties or through constant changes in schooling. Their wives find it difficult to establish friendly relations with neighbors. It is hardly surprising that the migrant cherishes a mental image of his homeland or

The people versus the machine.
Left: These two girls from Macá, in southern Chile, are victims of the head-on collision of their own and our mechanized culture. They have lost both their link with the past and control of the future.
Above: In South America, where traffic multiplies faster than the roads to carry it, people and automobiles live a split-level existence.

birthplace, though he seldom returns there. Being forced to move by continually changing local circumstances, he is as much a victim of future shock as were the gypsies who roamed Europe in earlier times.

David Kinefield

Mail-order mates

Man seeks woman, woman seeks man: that's the way it's always been. But it's a sad comment on our impersonal society that such an obvious need has to be advertised in a newspaper.

"Bouncing widow and three daughters, all in prime order and well-seasoned" offered themselves in the personal columns of a 1798 issue of the London *Times* to "any four broad-backed young fellows of spirit."

The use of personal columns to find interpersonal partners is a long-established practice. Then, as now, the partner may be required for any one of a number of things: for an evening's sexual activity—aberrant or normal, paid or unpaid—or merely for

someone to accompany the advertiser to places where it is fairly depressing to be alone—restaurants or theaters or on vacation—or, most seriously, for "friendship, view marriage."

"Lonely hearts" advertising for homosexuals covers much the same spectrum: from paid sexual activity through companionship without intended sexual activity to what may be described as "friendship, view stable cohabitation."

Where financial gain is involved in

personal advertisements, the advertiser may be either seller or buyer. One frequent buyer is the male advertiser—often impotent—who is willing to pay a female partner to participate in a generally repugnant form of aberrant sex. Such advertisements may ask for a "broadminded" or "funloving" respondent or even, confusingly, for one with a "sense of humor." The implication seems to be that any woman who likes "straight" sexual intercourse is a narrow-minded, humorless individual. The advertiser is likely to be an elderly, overweight, married, sexually inadequate man who has acquired a comfortable income but little liking for fellow humans.

A probable majority of fee-oriented advertisements are not offering any reward but seeking it. Apart from direct prostitution advertising and people offering aberrant sex for payment, there are those hoping to find a stable sexual partner who has a comfortable apartment or house where they might live. There is also the gigolo or the homosexual seeking a "take me out and about" partner—and females doing the same. She is of course doing something that is socially acceptable: when a man takes out a woman he pays for her, and no bargain about sexual activity is normally implied by her acceptance of such payment. The males seeking such a relationship are in a different position: being paid for makes it obligatory to consent to any required sexual activity.

Fortune Hunter
Sometimes a comprehensive form of gain is sought. The *New Statesman*, a British left-wing political weekly, has an incongruously extensive lonely hearts classified section. In an amusing advertisement headed "Good Fortune Hunter," an "energetic 70-year old widower" explained that he had recently emerged from "cherishing invalid wife for ten years" and was now lonely. He described himself as an atheist and humanist and a "still undiscovered" artist. He wanted a woman of culture and of "more than adequate means" who would "discover, organize, exploit, present comfort and cherish him both in his capacity as a man and as an artist." He would, he said, now like "to live well, eat well, travel well and to be, for a change, generally looked after."

Not all the men advertising for female service sound so attractively humorous and fair. A very reasonable-sounding advertisement read: "Professional man, own house in country, divorced, seeks mature, intelligent woman for friendship/marriage." An attractive 30-year-old journalist replied to it, giving her telephone number. He phoned her at 7 o'clock on a Sunday morning, told her in an overbearing voice that the house was full of food waiting to be cooked, cleaning and ironing needing to be done, and why didn't she come down at once and start on it? He seemed surprised that she did not find the offer tempting. When she suggested

that what he needed was a house-keeper, he exploded with wrath at the wages they demanded.

Demands abound for the common forms of female help—sexual or domestic service, and ego support. These pleas are sometimes couched in terms of great self-pity: "Chris, 35, living alone, used to fighting life's battles on his own, sensitive person, vulnerable, sad, angry" or "Shy, frustrated male, 24, misfit, seeks broad-minded, loving older woman."

One 36-year-old man utters a *cri de coeur* about his appearance: "I'm genuinely an attractive person but hair is thinning so if this horrifies keep clear." It does not, however, stop him from seeking someone much younger than he is. Men frequently demonstrate a capacity for self-deception about their age almost as great as women's—indefensible in a society in which a man may select a woman several decades younger than he is but a woman may not. A 24-year-old heads his advertisement "Boy, 24 . . ."; a 33-year-old heads his "Young guy...." One woman shows more realism and humor: "Cynical old lady (40) seeks man who enjoys life without excessive romantic fantasies."

There is a small minority of men frankly requiring financial support from women: a writer seeking "lady patron," an expensively educated man wanting "female with private income." On the other hand, there is a steady element of puritanism among the advertisers: "Bachelor, respectable, Protestant, 42, seeks clean-living, homely, single young lady . . . no divorcees/widows."

Mentally Unstable
The ways women deceive men in the ads are various. They lie endlessly about their age; they conceal the existence of children, especially if they have several; they will claim to be divorced when they are merely separated from their husband; and they may even claim to be separated when still living with him. Women teachers commonly conceal their occupation in the belief that it intimidates men and also because they fear that it might bring replies from male teachers, whom they often detest.

A common disappointment for men is that the women they encounter through these ads are often desperate for somebody to talk to. The personal column is very attractive to the mentally unstable, and certainly some of the compulsive talkers complained of by male respondents may be in need of professional therapy. But many

lonely women, especially those with small children, are simply so isolated by the conventions of our society that they become unaccustomed to personal contacts. This, together with nervousness about the unusual nature of their meeting, may impel them to overwhelm the man with chatter.

Immodest and Implausible
One difficulty about advertising for a partner, as distinct from going to an agency or bureau, is to hit upon a reasonable-sounding description of the partner you seek and, even more importantly, of yourself. A bachelor advertising for a "home-loving Christian spinster" in the 1970s would seem likely to provide a grim home life. Women describing themselves as "lovely" or "extremely attractive" sound immodest and vaguely implausible, as do men describing themselves as "extremely personable."

But the personal column has developed its own argot: one researcher found that he got no reply to the reasonable-sounding advertisement "Lonely but not unattractive gentleman would like to meet pleasing lady for companionship"; but he got many replies when he advertised "Writer, attractive, and in early forties would like to meet friendly girl." Almost everyone describes themselves as attractive in this game. It does not seem to devalue the description; it merely means that if you omit the word, it leads people to infer that you must be unsightly.

Many of the descriptions are oddly inadequate: someone will list music as a chief interest without specifying pop, rock, classic, opera, jazz or whatever. Others are explicit, if somewhat garrulous and showing an odd sense of values: "Witty girl journalist, Jewish (28), needs equally amusing, talented man interested in everything—maybe working in media or several business ventures. Share ideal intellectual glossy-magazine life-style." "Intellectual" and "glossy-magazine life-style" are normally mutually exclusive concepts, but she has made it clear that what she wants is a hustler and one with a highly polished life-style with intellectual pretensions, so the ad may very well work.

The greatest intentional deception arising from the ads is, however, sexual. Where the deception is the male's, it will usually be that he is concealing

There's no guarantee that the self-styled handsome hunk will match up to your expectations when you finally meet him in the flesh.

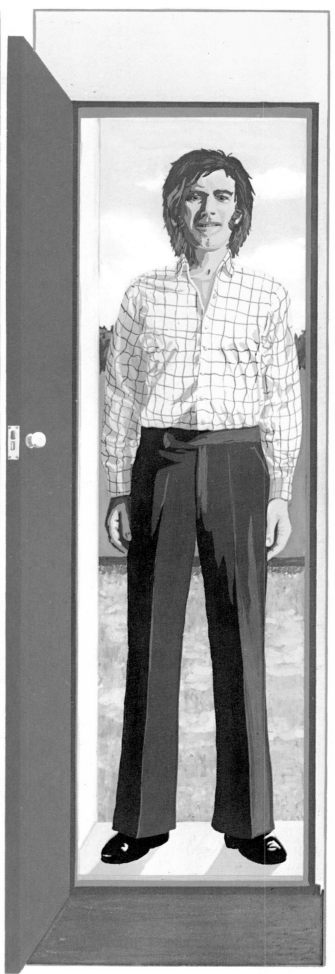

David Kinefield

the fact that it is not companionship but sex that he is seeking; or, if it is deviant sex he wants, he will intimate sex but not the deviation. Where the deception is the female's, it is usually that she is seemingly offering sex for free but actually wants payment for it.

The euphemisms employed are legion. Advertising managers of newspapers and magazines sometimes go to a great deal of trouble to learn the euphemisms and keep out those they particularly disapprove of, as well as those likely to flout the law. Some papers curiously reject ads from women wanting men but allow men to advertise for women. Quality newspapers may refuse to carry any lonely hearts ads at all. The customary euphemisms are often difficult to spot, and newspaper admen frequently pass a phrase only to learn of its sexual intent after the paper is published.

Well-known Euphemisms

A woman advertising for a businessman or a kindly or generous man is usually offering herself for a fee. "Occasional companionship," sought or offered, means sexual intercourse. "interested in amateur theater" means transvestism. Any reference to interest in education means corporal punishment, with or without bondage. Offers of sex to "mature man" intimates recognition of probable impotence. "Interested in photography" means nude posing or voyeurism. "Model" is of course the best-known euphemism for a prostitute, and "French lessons" and a variety of other language lessons all have their sexual meanings.

Even words like "enthusiastic," "sympathetic," and "understanding" have firm sexual connotations for those in the know. "Companionship, poss. marriage" may merely indicate the possibility of sexual intercourse.

The common word "bookkeeper" for prostitutes has led to countless misunderstandings. One elderly self-employed bookkeeper living near Soho, the red-light area of London, was naive enough to ask a local shop to put a card in the window advertising her availability to keep books and giving her telephone number. She was bewildered by the succession of lascivious voices calling her up and asking about the bookkeeping she did.

Women answering apparently straightforward ads are often dismayed by almost spontaneous demands for sex and by the advertiser's incredulity that they did not understand the sexual meaning of the ad. But men, too, often do not understand this esoteric language. One

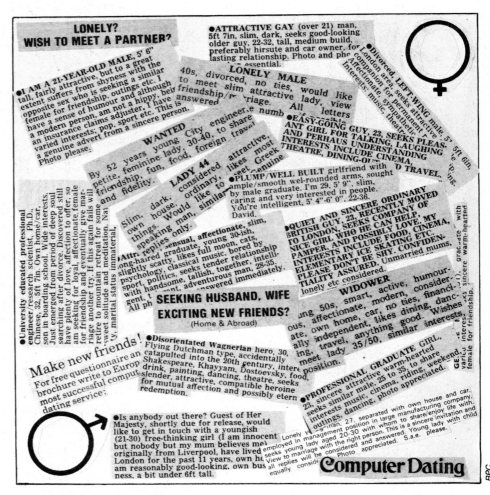

woman advertiser found that several of her respondents expressed great relief at her nonsexual behavior—they had been bewildered by contacts with women who offered not companionship but sex, usually for payment.

The most intellectual papers sometimes carry the most exploitive ads, treating women as packages of flesh, even while wanting them intelligent and socially presentable as well. An ad that begins "Senior international official, 43, seeks cultured, mature female, with university background, for marriage. Replies only from women with high degree of physical and personal charm" goes on to give exact specifications of the permitted height (5 feet 4-7 inches) and even weight (130-145 pounds).

Although a majority of women in most personal columns are after companionship rather than sexual encounters, there are some magazines in which this is reversed. Contact magazines are frankly concerned with women (and to some extent with men) as packages of flesh. "Very pretty blonde offers intimate friendship in her warm cosy home to considerate gentleman . . . must be clean and uninhibited." Few of the women advertising in contact magazines are after sex itself, without

Someone, somewhere, wants you. It seems that every preference is catered for in lonely hearts ads.

a fee for it; in this ad the word "considerate" certainly means "for a consideration." Some women's ads claim to be "genuine first ad" or "noncommercial" but men replying have found no noncommercial contacts at all. Virtually every advertisement in contact magazines is made by a prostitute—or a prostitute's agent. Here deceit about age can be bizarre: 45 may mean 60; "youngish" may mean 70.

Wildly Contorting

Contact magazines are illustrated with unskilled photographs of naked women (including one disarmingly pleasant lady sitting comfortably in unprovocative panties, looking more like an absentminded curate's wife than a hustling prostitute). There are also photographs showing couples in apparent sexual intercourse. There are close-ups of women's genitals but, significantly, none of men's—partly because the magazines are aimed principally at men; partly because the purpose of the photographs would be defeated by the demonstrably unexcited state of the males in the photographs; and partly, probably, because

dator is probably the norm among personal column advertisers: sexual or financial or moral predators, demanding service without involvement. It might be more realistic to call what goes on in these columns "intersexual bargaining"—with the bargaining conducted, as is usual, in the currencies or terms in use by each sex.

At the same time, many advertisers and respondents merit compassion, like neurotics and variously handicapped people. For understandable reasons, some of them use the columns as a way of manipulating people, often displaying a kind of punishing arrogance at encounters. One man of 60 who was only 4 feet 8 inches tall (and who had failed to mention these facts when he answered a woman's ad), was full of authority when they met by arrangement in a hotel bar, briskly telling her at once that he was afraid that he could not stay because he had arranged to meet another lady in another bar in the hotel. Telling her with rapid approval that she was beautiful, he complained bitterly to her about the physical attributes of the last lady he had met—she had been fat and not young enough, he said indignantly, as he left with a condescending nod.

photographs of sexually excited males are considered more obscene than the most wildly contorting females. And male models capable of erection to order probably come more expensive than the contact magazines are prepared to budget for.

Deviations are plentifully catered for in these magazines: bisexuality, group sex, couples advertising for another couple; a wife seeking an additional man ("husband approves" or "husband present"—a near-impotent husband may masturbate while watching his wife in bed with the other man).

A male describes himself as wanting to "submit to every whim of a dominant female"; a woman offers herself as "lovely kinky blonde pussy"; a "33-year-old offers her services to mature gentleman . . . spanking enthusiasts welcome." Not every woman is prepared to do everything. There are many ads like "nothing too way-out for me," and an occasional "no kinks or perverts" appears. It is difficult to discover what may or may not be regarded as kinky, however. One man describing himself as "not kinky," then went on to explain that he wanted a woman who was a "keen oralist, would dress in suspenders, etc., for sex," and that they would together visit other "funloving" people where

Looking in the "wanted" column of a newspaper may be the last resort in the quest for romance.

she would be "Shown off as my wife."

The personal column companionship ads, on the whole, are inhabited by takers, not givers. (Contact magazine prostitutes can hardly be said to be either: they are merely in business.) Most of the men are seeking sexual encounters that absolve them of any need to invest affection or involvement. Many others are asking for therapy. They are saying, in effect, "I have told you that I am shy/hurt/angry, now take over—assuage me, boost my ego, look after me."

Lazy Predator

The women are probably a little better. Because our society limits women in the ways they may, without censure, approach men, there are more women who genuinely seek companionship, with sex occurring naturally if and when mutual attraction occurs. The women are marginally more likely to be prepared to work a little at their encounters and are probably increasingly willing to pay their way financially, despite being conditioned to believe it unfeminine.

But, with either sex, the lazy pre-

Hope Chest

Report after report indicates a very high failure rate for anyone using personal columns in an attempt to find a likable or lovable partner, with much resulting pain. It is undoubtedly true that a person with a strong and competent personality could, with perseverance, eventually encounter a few people who were neither neurotic nor exploitive. But with so small an incidence of these, it is unlikely that he would find someone with shared interests. And if he were so strong and competent and persevering, he would hardly need to resort to such methods to find a partner.

Many respondents have no intention of doing more than chatting on the phone with someone and perhaps arranging a tentative meeting. They may spend a lot of enjoyable time each week simply replying to ads, without ever following through. And many advertisers enjoy scanning the letters they get, toying with the idea of answering them. They may advertise whenever they feel depressed, relishing each batch of replies, regarding them as a sort of ever-renewable hope chest. On the whole, that seems to be as constructive a way as any to use the personal columns.

Coping with insecurity

Maybe there was a golden age when everyone felt secure. But even when society was more structured, there was war, disease, and unpredictable famine to contend with—insecurity seems to be part of the human condition. But does that mean that all we can do is suffer?—optimism is also part of human nature. Perhaps the secret of living is to escape from needless insecurity and to be optimistic whenever the situation warrants it.

How Insecure are You?

Successful people are often motivated by insecurity. Beautiful women frequently suffer doubts about their attractiveness. How many people do you know who appear to have everything and yet are crippled by lapses of confidence? Check out the degree of insecurity you feel and the sorts of occasion in which it crops up.

1. When others criticize your actions, do you react
a. with indifference?
b. with some uneasiness?
c. with hurt or angry responses?
2. If you very much want to make a good impression on someone, do you
a. find it easy to talk to him and show warmth?
b. feel frightened and tense but make the attempt to communicate?
c. feel so nervous that you let your opportunities go?
3. On a plane flight, one of the engines develops trouble. Would you
a. assume that you'll land safely?
b. feel decidedly alarmed but tell yourself that statistically your chances are pretty good?
c. spend the rest of the journey in a panic?
4. Are you frightened of situations that most people cope with easily, like crossing bridges, using elevators, or finding yourself in closed spaces or crowds?
a. not in the least
b. only if you feel tired or upset
c. frequently
5. How do you feel when someone is angry with you?
a. calm and reasonable
b. a little flustered and worried
c. terrified
6. When a relationship is going well, do you
a. enjoy it?
b. sometimes worry about what would happen if it broke up?
c. hold back in case it might end?
7. If you are alone in an unfamiliar

place, do you
a. go ahead and explore it?
b. feel less comfortable than in your usual surroundings but try to get something out of it?
c. feel totally lost and want to run away?
8. When you meet someone that you take a liking to and he reveals that he holds views that differ from yours on a matter important to you, do you
a. accept that difference makes life interesting?
b. start to like him less?
c. feel anxious and rush to defend your opinion?
9. Do you fear that if people knew you as you really are they would reject you?
a. never
b. sometimes
c. most of the time
10. When someone you respect praises what you have done, do you
a. feel unmixed pleasure?
b. feel grateful but wonder if you really deserve it?
c. suspect that he is only being kind?

The Origins of Insecurity

All human beings run the risk of feeling insecure in their early years. A baby is almost entirely at the mercy of those around him, and even when they are well-disposed they will not always be able to gratify his needs instantly. The eminent psychoanalyst Erik Erikson sees infancy as crucial in forming a basic attitude of trust or mistrust, towards both the world and yourself.

What is important is not that every experience should be a good one but that the overall balance should be weighted towards optimism. For all kinds of reasons this does not always happen: inherited temperament, for example, may make some children more vulnerable to bad experiences. But the distinguishing characteristic of human beings is our capacity to go on learning. Reversing the lessons of early experience—of feeling repulsive and worthless—can take time, but it can be done.

Then and Now

Without our awareness, old behavior patterns keep operating: a successful adult may feel like a helpless child inside. To free yourself from the past, you need to recognize first of all just what it is that you are feeling. Then you need to sort out realistic sources of insecurity from the leftover, inappropriate patterns of the past. In his dealings with patients, psychotherapist Carl Rogers found that many of them needed permission to be them-

selves. The child often has to shape himself to adult expectations and abandon his real self: no wonder he feels insecure and confused. Without going into therapy, you can start to help yourself. No adult is in fact as powerless as the child he feels himself.

Value Yourself

The adult part of you can appraise your real achievements and qualities and acknowledge that your faults are not so very bad. What is it about you that is so awful? Maybe you get jealous, or greedy, or need assurance, but who doesn't? Whose approval do you want, anyway? Many people who suffer from insecurity were unable to gain love in childhood unless they behaved as their parents wished. Is that your problem? It's time to set your own standards instead of clinging to impossible demands.

Acting Secure

Deceiving yourself about your feelings usually leads to disaster, but, if you know what you are doing, pretending to be more secure than you feel can go a long way towards overcoming your fears. All you need is the courage to take the first step.

How Do You Rate?

Mainly as—insecurity would not seem to be a problem for you. If you have answered honestly, you are lucky in your temperament or upbringing. Look carefully at any b or c score that you have—it could show an area where you are less confident than usual. In dealings with others, remember that they do not always share your security and so may come across as withdrawn or overaggressive.

Mainly bs—you could be hampered in some aspects of your life by feelings of insecurity. If you gave b as the response to question 3, this shows a normal reaction to a situation of real danger. The other b responses indicate that you do not allow insecurity to curb your action but that you could be more comfortable in many social situations with a stronger sense of your own worth. Mainly cs—for you insecurity is a real problem. Whatever you achieve, you are haunted by the feeling that you will be found out. Personal relationships may crack under the strain of your unspoken demands. If you can develop a better view of yourself, your life could be changed dramatically.

Saying Goodbye

Carl Rogers, the originator of client-centered therapy and one of the most important psychologists in the field of personal growth through encounter groups, believes that the capacity to form close relationships quickly, then to let them go without regrets, is vital in today's society.

Yet most of us prize, at least as an ideal, permanent, dependable relationships. Stemming from the extreme dependency of human infants, we have a need to hold on to those we love. When love fails, whatever the reason, pain is inevitable, but with honesty and care two people can avoid bitterness and help heal each other's pain.

Rarely do two people fall out of love at the same time, so there is often one who wants to go and one who does not want to be abandoned. Sympathy is usually given to the one who is left, but being the one to go is tough too. You have to accept the guilt of hurting someone else, and it can be easier to be the victim than the aggressor. How do you cope?

Defensive Reactions
Most couples, when they are splitting up, go through a period of blaming each other. We all are geared to preserve a good self-image, and reason does not come into it. Try, as far as you can, to stop blaming and defending. That can become a vicious circle, damaging to both of you. You have both made mistakes. Listen to what your partner says, and then weigh up, privately and calmly, how true the accusations are. If you don't want to make the same mistakes again, treat it as a learning opportunity.

A common defense is to close communication. If you are inclined to cut and run, you might ask yourself where that gets you? Out of a difficult situation in the short term, but what about the next time? It could be that your refusal to listen was one of the things that spoiled this relationship; if you don't find out what went wrong, you could spend your life moving from one bad scene to another.

Justifying your wish to go is another defense. The only answer is to take responsibility for your own actions. The line between selfishness and doing what you must is sometimes unclear. Maybe you have wanted to go for some time, but were afraid to leave the other person in an emotional mess; maybe you stayed because you had young children—an excellent reason for trying to make the best of things, so long as the children do not suffer more from the stresses of a bad marriage.

Don't expect your wishes to be absolutely clear all of the time. Nostalgia and guilt will make you wonder what you really want. But if you are in touch with your own feelings, there comes a time when you are certain, on balance, that you have to go.

Honesty is the Best Policy
Once you know that it is over, be honest. However frail or dependent your partner may be, it is easier to cope with the truth than live through a cycle of hope and despair. On the pretext of not hurting the other one, it is all too possible to inflict much greater cruelty. Be straight with yourself and with your partner—accept that your going will cause pain—do what you can to help, then get out.

Rejection calls into question our personal worth. You can't walk out on someone without damaging his image; but try to leave him with some self-respect. If the only way your partner can keep his sense of self intact is to get furiously angry with you, initially, then you have to put up with it. Later on there will be more chance for a balanced view to grow.

You cannot take responsibility *for* others—that is depriving them of the right to live their own life. But you can act in a responsible way without being patronizing. You could be surprised by the success with which your old partner takes up a new life. In any case, it will cease to be your business.

If You Are Left
Hate, anger, misery—you will probably go through them all. It can help, at first, to shout, scream, cry and protest. Use your friends—you've helped them before. Whatever you do, don't sink into private despair, but take positive action to assert your worth. Once the time of uncertainty is over, you may alternate between hostility and self-doubt. Maybe you will feel resentful of the efforts you made to keep the relationship going. And maybe you are right to feel badly treated.

Right or not, you have to face the fact of life without your old partner. Grief is a healthy reaction, as long as it does not go on too long. Freud pointed out in *Mourning and Melancholia* that depression stemming from natural grief at a real loss can go on beyond the time when it should have healed, though allowing yourself to feel sad, oddly enough, is ultimately healing. Mourning rituals, found in every society but our own, acknow-ledge the right of a bereaved person to express sorrow. Don't try to be too brave too early. In time, the hurt grows less: the pain may be just as sharp, but it comes less frequently.

It is impossible to say how long natural mourning takes. To get over a deep and important relationship can take up to two years, but a few weeks should see you through the worst stage. If you don't seem to be getting any better, seek professional help. It could be that you invest too much in others because you have a weak sense of your own worth. If you can build up your own strength, future relationships will be more rewarding and more lasting.

Creative Separation
When communication between two people breaks down, they can become damaging and restrictive to each other. One feeling that may take you by surprise on separation is *relief*: short-term relief from the quarrels and anxieties and the long-term possibility of being more of your own person. It is particularly difficult for women, especially when they are no longer young, to adjust to the freedom of acting on their own wishes and insights.

At first, the freedom may seem empty, but by degrees you can get in touch with what you want and start to lead your own life instead of backing up someone else's. Rushing into a new relationship sometimes helps, but not if you repeat the old mistakes. Get to know yourself, then you will be more ready to relate on a healthy basis with someone else. It is no accident that so many marriages and love affairs are usually much better the second time around.

Hello, good-bye, hello . . .

How's your aim?

Success depends on many things besides ability—opportunity, perseverance, and what you expect of yourself. Most of us never operate to capacity. Are you setting your sights too low? Or are you setting your sights too high? If you go the opposite way and expect too much too soon, you will probably give up out of frustration.

The Expectation Effect

The American psychologists Rosenthal and Jacobson made an odd discovery in the late 1960s. They gave sets of identical rats to their students, but told one group that their rats had been specially bred for intelligence and the other that their rats were particularly dull. Then both sets of students carried out routine learning experiments with the animals. The "dull" rats learned more slowly; the "bright" ones more quickly—yet they were of identical heredity!

Moreover, the students with the supposedly "intelligent" rats reported that they enjoyed working with them and were seen to handle them more. Clearly some kind of expectation effect was at work.

What Are Your Expectations?

Self-expectation stems from the expectations of others. Tell a kid he's dumb from an early age, and he will probably prove you right. Conversely, tell him that he is bright, and he will attempt more, and raise his aspiration level. Are you still under the influence of early expectations? Do you assume that you are good at some things, bad at others? Have you recently given yourself a chance at the things you think you cannot do? Or do you hold back from trying new activities in case you fail?

Test Your Aspiration

To get some idea of how you set and alter what you think you can do, give half an hour to this experiment. Choose a task that is not too difficult, but which is slightly unfamiliar to you. Men might try threading a needle; women might mend a fuse.

1. CHOOSE THE TASK AND SET YOUR GOAL. How many successes do you expect to have in 10 minutes?
2. PRACTICE FOR 10 MINUTES. RECORD YOUR RESULTS. How well do your goals and your achievements match?
3. NOW RESET YOUR GOALS. How many successes do you expect in 10 minutes?

4. PRACTICE FOR ANOTHER TEN MINUTES. Compare results with your goal. If you have the patience, repeat for a third time.

Rate Your Performance

First aspiration level. If you set more goals than you achieved, give yourself +1 for each expected success. If you set fewer goals than you actually achieved, give yourself −1 for each goal underset.
Second and third aspiration level. Give yourself +2 or −2 for over- and undersetting goals.

Minus Scores

A minus score does not necessarily mean that you habitually underestimate yourself at the first level. Not knowing what to expect can lead to error. But if you continued to predict less success than you achieved, you are fooling yourself. Why? Check off the reason(s) for continuing to underset your goals:
1. You learned faster than you expected.
2. You prefer to set low goals so that you will feel good when you do better than you said.
3. You were afraid that you wouldn't achieve much.
4. You like to be cautious until you're sure of yourself.
How far do these reasons apply to other aspects of your life?

Plus Scores

Again, an initial overestimation is not necessarily significant, but continued high aspiration is. Was there a better match between prediction and achievement by the third attempt? If not, you could be setting your aspiration level too high. Check off any reason(s) for high goal setting.
1. You thought the task was easy.
2. You always think big.
3. You need a spur to keep you trying hard.
4. You carried out the experiment in competition with someone else.
Do any of these reasons ring a bell about your general behavior?

If you gave up, was it because the task was too easy or too difficult?

If you went on beyond three trials, was it to match your goal, out of sheer determination?

Accurate goal setting after the first trial could mean that you have a realistic level of aspiration or that you satisfy yourself with what you decide to do. It isn't, of course, foolproof to generalize from a small experiment: you are the only one who can tell just how much it says about your approach.

Inhibition, Complacence and High Hopes

To find out more generally how you set your goals, check which of the following statements are true for you.
1. I am often afraid to try things if I think I will not succeed.
2. I often find that I have taken on more than I can do.
3. I know my capacities pretty well.
4. I have been surprised at times to find that I can do something I never thought I could.
5. I often dream about the things I could accomplish.
6. I do my best in all situations.
7. When I'm criticized, I stop trying.
8. When I'm criticized, I try harder.
9. I would rate myself fairly successful in most of the things I've done.
10. I know I could do a lot more if I had the right opportunities.
11. I am afraid of failure, even when I know what to do.
12. I do not expect to fail when I know what to do.

Rate Your Confidence

Inhibition. Yes answers to questions 1 and 4 give you **3** each; yes to questions 7 and 11 gives you **5** each.
Even a low score in this area should make you stop to think. You underrate yourself. Do you know why? It could be that you were given a bad image of yourself in early life or that success is too important to you. To escape from the anxiety of failing, you prefer not to try. You need to develop more confidence and a toleration of failure.

Complacence. Yes answers to questions 3, 6, 9 and 12 give you **3** each. Satisfaction with your accomplishments could be a good thing, unless, of course, your satisfaction is another way of avoiding anxiety. Perhaps you are making the best of small achievements when you could do much better. If you are really happy with your success, you will not need to do anything about it. If there is some doubt in your mind, raise your aspirations.

High hopes. Yes answer to question 8 gives you **3**; yes to questions 2, 5 and 10 gives you **5** each.
An unrealistically high aspiration level can lead to disappointment and the abandonment of effort. But if your dreams and your optimism keep you trying, don't give them up. You are more likely to succeed than inhibited or complacent people, if you have the persistence to bring your actual performance closer to your high expectations.

and B.F. Skinner, 419-21
and hysteria, 926
in psychotherapy, 424
see also Skinner, B.F.,
Bell, Jeffrey, 349
Belson, Dr. W. A., on violence, 1298
Bentham, Jeremy, on criminal reform, 1097
berdache, *see* transvestism
Berg, Prof. Paul, on genetic engineering, 1432, 1435
Berger, Hans, 153
discovery of EEG, 565-6
Bergson, Henri (philosopher), 689, 789, 1512
Beria, Laurenti, 683
Berkeley, George (philosopher), 1512
Bernard, Jessie, 196
egalitarian marriage, 972
emancipation, 767-8
working wives, 440
Berne, Dr. Eric, 265, 1026
smiling, 2652
transaction analysis, 1983, 1985
Bernstein, Carl, on Watergate, 1330
Berry, Chuck, 1968, *1940*
Berscheid, Ellen, 69
on social intercourse, 2652
Besant, Annie, 795, 796
Theosophical Society, 2593
bestiality, 203, 1512
sexual taboo on, 1648
Bettelheim, Bruno, institutional child rearing, 2882
Beyond Freedom and Dignity (B. F. Skinner), 421, 424
Beyond Telepathy (A. Puharich), 755
Bible, The, as best seller, 2735-6
bibliokleptomania, 1513
bigamy, problems of, 1342-3
see also marriage
Binet, Alfred, 84
study of intelligence, 457, 1513
biochemistry, 1514
biocybernetics, 1514
biofeedback, 1514
techniques of, 2103-7
use of, 2130-33
biogenetics, 1514
see also evolution
biological time mechanism, *see* body rhythm
biological warfare, 2584-5
see also chemical warfare, war
biometry, 1514
biosphere, 1514
Bird of Paradise, The (R. D. Laing), 858
Birney, Dr. R. C., on scholastic achievement, 1737
birth,
cloaca theory, 1642
couvade, 1706
rebirth fantasy, 2249
superstition surrounding, 145
timing of, 129
trauma, 1514
birth control, *see* contraception
Bismarck, Count, 1024
bisexuality,
definition of, 1548
and marriage, 1070
problems of, 1069-73
Black Box, use in radiesthesia, 1103, 1104, 1105, 1107, 1548, *1106*
Blaiberg, Dr. Philip, 1422-3
Blair, Prof. T. (environmentalist), on urban density, 1466
Blanco, Juan (faith healer), 816
Blavatsky, Madame, and Theosophical Society, 2593
Bleuler, Eugen (psychiatrist), 1548
blindness, psychic, 2246
Blood, Robert, on marriage, 1427
blood group, 1548
Blyth, Chay, 548, 550, 551

body,
abdomen, 1344
alimentary canal, 1384
amino acids in, 1385
antibodies in, 1407
antigen, 1407
appetites of, 1408
arrested development of, 1472
bilateral symmetry in, 1513
cerebrospinal fluid, 1614
cranium, 1706
deformation of, 1755-6
female attractiveness, 70
fitness of, 1191-2
genetic engineering, 2837
image, 1549
language,
eye contact, 1090
and group therapy, 1093
incidence of, 1089
posture, 1134
proxemics, 1132-3
rules of, 1090
signalling by, 1134, 1549
smiling, 1090-2
male,
attractiveness of, 2596-7
development of, 2837, 2839
muscle,
asynergia of, 1474
atonicity of, 1474
atrophy of, 1474
physical tension in, 1077-8
psychological approach to, 1077
rhythm, 129-33
of astronauts, 993
and health, 133
normal, 990-91
and shift work, 130
and travel, 991-3
type,
asthenic, 1473
athletic, 1474, 2289-93
body building,
Associations for, 2733
and Charles Atlas, 2730-33
contests, 2734
George Hackenschmidt, 2732-3
Body Image and Personality (Fisher and Cleveland), 1292

Body Language (Dr. Julius Fast), 1134
Bond, Dr. Douglas, 1769, 1770
Bonesana, Cesare, prison reform, 1097
Bono, Edward de, lateral thinking, 1558
books, best-selling, 2735-8
boss,
background of, 182
isolation of, 181
personality of, 180
woman as, 184
see also dominance
Boston, Richard, 2011
Botkin, S. P., 330
Boulding, Kenneth, on future shock, 2840
Boulting, Roy, *236*
Bow, Clara, 1873-4
Bowlby, John, 1761
mourning, 2274, 2275
social responsiveness of child, 1484, 1485
Boyd, Dr. W. E., 1104, 1106, 1107
Boys and Sex (Dr. W. B. Pomeroy), 2211
Bradlaugh, Charles, 795, 796
braggart, character of, 898-900
Braid, J., and mesmerism, 296, 298, 895, 896
braille, 1549
brain,
aggression center in, 1363
alpha rhythm of, 154, 1384
of amphioxus, 1386
amygdala in, 1386
arousal of, 1472
association cortex in, 1473
beta wave in, 1513
betz cells in, 1513
binocular fusion in, 1513
binocular rivalry in, 1513-14
blood-brain barrier, 1548
center of activation, 1346
cerebellum, 275, 277, 1590
cerebral dominance, 1614
cerebrum, 1614
communication within, 408
construction of, 153-7, 1549
see also under individual sub-entries
cybernetics and, 167
damage, 443
apraxia result of, 1408
ataxia, 1474
Bender-Gestalt test, 1512
Delgado's work on, 172-4

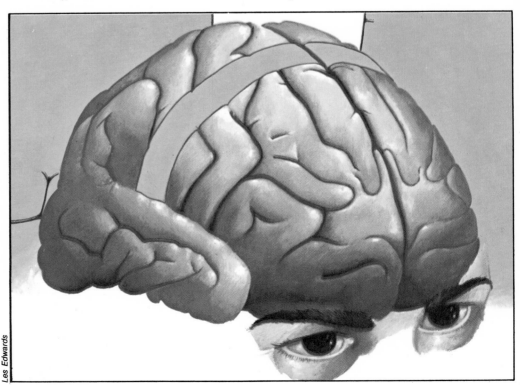
Les Edwards

effect of psychedelic drugs on, 408-9
executive area of, 1884
experiments on, 168-71
focussing ability of, 1488
   span of, 2340
forebrain, 1911
frontal lobe, 1948
functions of, 163
future development of, 2839
gray matter, 1979
gyrus, 1979
hemisphere, 2004
   hemispherical dominance, 2004
higher centers, 2004
hindbrain, 2004
hippocampus, 2004
hypothalamus, 1782, 2007
and intelligence, 458
interbrain, 2030
language center, 2075
lateral dominance, 2075
lesion, 1549
and memory, 277-81
midbrain, 2126
occipital cortex, 2151
parietal, 2193
perversion of, 2839
rhinencephalon, 2266
rhythm in, 2130-33
speech center, 2340
stimulation of, 412, 1550
storage, 1550
storm, 1550
surgery, 173
   lobotomy, 166, 1948
   psychosurgery, 1009-12
temporal lobe, 2367
visual cortex, 2394
waves, 1550
at work, 158-62
Brain, Memory and Learning (W. R. Russell), 285
brainwashing, and sensory deprivation, 743, 1550
Branch, Margaret, and gifted children, 864
Brando, Marlon, 835, 1897
swearing, 2263
youth revolution, 1940, *1943*
Brazelton, Dr. Berry, 1623
Brazendale, Tony, 69
Break Down the Walls (John Martin), 1741
breath holding, 1550
Brecher, Edward, M., 501
breeding, selective, 2312-13
see also genetics
Breggin, Dr. Peter, 1009, 1012
Brennan, Michael, 1307
Brenton, Myran, on male role, 1954
Breuer, Joseph, 1550
broadcasting, power of, 1332-3
see also television
Broca, Paul, 164, 2204
speech area, 164, 2204
Bronowski, Dr. Jacob, 1416
Brookes-Smith, Colin, on psychokinesis, 1154, 1155
Brown, Dr. Daniel, on sexual monotony, 1317
Brown, James, on working conditions, 1833
Brown, Rapp, and New Left, 2303, 2306
Bruch, Dr. Hilde (child psychiatrist), 1581

Bruner, Jerome, 284, 1551
child's mind, 1794
bruxism, 1551
Bryan, William, 223
Buling, Hans, *1255*
Bull, Peter, 315
Bullough, Prof. William, 1410
Bunyan, John, 430
Burchett, George, tattooist, 2471
bureaucracy, inefficiency of, 2379
Burt, Prof. Sir Cyril, 611, 1551
gifted children, 862, 864
Burton, Sir Richard, 914-18
Burton, Richard, 89
Byrne, Mr. Justice, on pornography, 703
Byrne, Patrick, 1739-40, *1740*
Bywater, Freddy, 1712

C

Cajal, Santiago Ramon y, 303
Calder, Nigel, on yoga, 2654, 2655
Calhoun, John B., 135
studies of overcrowded rats, 2181
calligraphy, 1551
Calnan, James (plastic surgeon), 2410
Camber, Dr. Bernard, on driving, 1578
Campbell, Virginia, on poltergeists, 628-9

cancer,
controlling, 2792-3, 2795
death from, 2792
development of, 2791-2
types of, 2794-5
cannabis, *see* drugs
Cannon, Walter B. (psychologist), on physiology of emotion, 1551
cantharides, *see* aphrodisiac
capitalism,
Marx on, 2454-7
power and, 2476-9
Capra, Frank, 1826
cardiograph, *see* electrocardiograph
Carington, Whately, 1061
ESP, 1225
Carlile, Richard, 745-6
Carlyle, Thomas, on revenge, 1097
Carmichael, Stokeley, and New Left, 23-4, 2303, 2306
Carnegie, Dale, 2571
on ingratiation, 2652
Carrel, Dr. Alexis, 1104
Carrington, Hereward, psychic research, 1156
Carroll, Lewis, 1453
Carry on Talking (Peter Bander), 1307
Carson, Sir Edward, 402
Carson, Rachel, 1019, 2234
Carter, Robert, 926
cartomancy, 933
Case for Astrology, The (West and Tooner), 1006
Casson, Dr. F. R. C., on gambling, 652
Castaneda, Carlos, 215, 433, 708
techniques of awareness, 2519
Castle, Barbara, and TUC, 1732
castration,
anxiety, 1588
complex, 34, 1588

Spectrum

KEY TO INDEX

Major entries are in bold type and minor entries in light type. To find a reference first locate it under its first letter (e.g. s for **sex**). Entries are sometimes subdivided (e.g. **sex**, enjoyment of, 2370-73). A *see also* italic entry indicates additional information. Major book, film and play entries are in ***bold italics***. Major book entries appear as follows—e.g. ***Unknown Self, The*** (George Groddeck), 258. *Italic* page number entries mean a picture.

delinquent, 810, 1756
 juvenile, 2074, 2116-20
delirium, 1756
delirium tremens, 1756
 see also alcoholism
delusion, 1756
cynonthropy, 1728
of grandeur, 1756
mignon, 2126
Dement, William, 1756
dementia, 1756
praecox, *see* schizophrenia
senile, 2314
DeMille, Cecil B., 1825, 1898, *1824*
democracy,
and police, 2348
power within, 2782-4, 2785, 2786
demonology, 1756-7
demonomania, 1757
demophobia, 1757
 see also phobia
dependency, 1757
in children, 1790-93, 2778-81
depersonalization, 1757
depression, 1757
agitated, 1363
apathy in, 1408
depressive neurosis, 1757
depressive reaction, 1781
severe and ECT, 110
ways of alleviating, 2036-7
dermatitis, 1781
occupational disease, 2771-2
DeSalvo, Albert (Boston Strangler), 1594
Descartes, René, 133, 303, 1781
on robot, 2705
Descent of Man, The (Charles Darwin), 225
Deschooling Society (Ivan Illich), 2330
Dessoir, Max, 189
determinism, 1781
psychic, 2246
Deverson, Jane, homogamy in marriage, 1710
deviation, 1782
standard, 2341
see also sexual deviation
Devlin, Lord, on pornography, 662
Dewar, Diana, 2176
dexterity, 1782
dextrility, 1782
dextrosinistral, 1782
dianetics, theory of, 2619-20
Dianetics: The Modern Science of Mental
 Health (L. R. Hubbard), 2619
Dichter, Ernest, on male character, 2686
Dickens, Charles, on working children, 1990
dieting,
advisability of, 1247
and chewing gum, 1277
and cheese, 1278-9
and constipation, 1277
diabetic foods, 1277
difficulty of, 1246-7
and drugs, 1247-9
and honey, 1249
and hypnosis, 1279
rate of, 1249
and smoking, 1279
sweet foods, 1277
ways of, 1247
and yoghourt, 1249
Difference Between a Man and a Woman, The
 (Theo Lang), 1674
diffusion, 1782
Dingwall, Dr. Eric, 1107
Dion, Karen, 69
dipsomania, *see* alcoholism
discipline, 1783
and child, 2139-42
Discovery of Witchcraft (Reginald Scot), 536
discrimination, racial, and Negro, 1763
see also anti-semitism
disease, 1783
congenital,

anencephaly, 1387
 in children, 1270-71
discovery of, 2049
occupational, 2769-73
prevention by screening, 2445
Diseases of Workers (Bernardino Ramazzini),
 2770
disorientation, 1783
displacement, 1783
adjustment strategy, 2452
disseminated sclerosis, *see* sclerosis, multiple
dissociation, 1783
see also hypnosis
Divided Self, The (R. D. Laing), 856
divination, 1783
in animals, 1062
dowsing, 1062, 1124, 1170-73, 1827
 divining rod, 1783
of future,
 by ceromancy, 1614
 by crystal gazing, 1727
 by pendulum, 1104
divorce, 89
ease of, 571
problems of, 953-4, 955
reasons for, 1644–7, 2068-71
and remarriage, 954, 1013-16
and woman,
 antipathy of, 438-9
 initiated by, 951-3
see also child, love, marriage
Dix, Dorothea, 1783
Dixon, Jeanette, 981, 982
Dobzhansky, Dr. T., 1819
doctor, relationship with patient, 1460-62,
 1479-82
Dodds, Prof. E. R., 757
Dodgson, Charles, *see* Carroll, Lewis
Dollard, Dr. J., on aggression, 40
Doman, Glenn, 448
dominance, 111-15
automobile and, 1574-8
definition of, 112-13, 1827
establishing, 114
hierarchy of, 114-15, 137
incidence of, 113, 134
POW's and, 134-5
women and, 136
see also aggression, boss
Dominian, Dr. Jack, 1314
Doors of Perception, The (Aldous Huxley), 215,
 531
Douglas, Mary, and misogyny, 1497
Douglas, Judge William O., *702*
Dr. Spock Talks to Mothers (Dr. Benjamin
 Spock), 379, 2220
drama,
exercises in, 838-9
psychodrama, 839
dream, 9
compositive figure in, 1658
compression of, 1658
daydream, 18, 1728
day residue in, 1755
definition of, 1827
difference in male/female, 20
and ESP, 385
interpretation of, 13, 14, 19, 716-17
 latent content of, 2075
 symbol in, 14, 15-17, 19-22
origin of stress, 95
precognition in, 18, 1223-7
and psychotherapy, 149
and reality, 11, 12, 13
variety of, 10
waking, 2395
drive, 1827-8
drive reduction theory, 1828
Droscher, Vitus, 1062
drug,
addiction, 572-3
 and crime, 618
 and students, 2259

administration of, 133
demorphinization, 1757
effects of,
 on brain disease, 173
 on mind, 530
 side effects, 533-4
 on stress, 95
and heredity, 619
improves intelligence, 458
legality of, 553
overdose, 620-1
and psychotherapy, 110
reasons for taking, 552
resistance to antibiotics, 2418-21
trials, 2223-6
types of, 529-30
 amphetamine, 1386, 1512
 analgesic, 573-4
 antidepressant, 1407
 aspirin, 1346, 1473
 atropine, 1474
 barbiturate, 110, 1490
 benzodiazepine compounds, 1512
 caffeine, 1551
 cannabis, 553, 1551
 chloroform, 1616
 cocaine, 1642
 codeine, 1643
 datura, 215
 dextroamphetamine (Dexedrine), 1782
 dilantin, 1782
 dramamine, 1827
 hallucinogen, 531
 plant drugs, 213-16
 sedative, 530-31, 1616
Drysdale, Dr. George, 747, 796
Dual-Career Families (Rhona and Robert
 Rapoport), 766
dualism, 1828
Duchamp, Marcel, and surrealism, 2755,
 2756
Dunne, J. W., 18
precognition, 1223, 1224
Durrant, Elizabeth, on stepchild, 2327-8
Duvalier, 'Papa Doc', and voodoo, 503, 596,
 598, *504*
dwarfism, 1828
and achondroplasia, 1346
Dying (John Hinton), 2110, 2145
Dylan, Bob, 1973
dynamometer, 1828
dysgraphia, 1828
dyslexia, 1828
cause of, 2535-6
incidence of, 2533-5
remedial training, 2536

E ear, 524-5
 auricle of, 1488-9
 basilar membrane of, 1490
 bone conduction to, 1549
 cochlea of, 1642
 eustachian tube, 1884
external auditory meatus, 1885
function of, 525-7, 1828
hammer, 1980
incus, 2028
inner, 2029
labyrinth, 2074
middle, 2126
and music, 528
noise fatigue, 528
scalar tympani, 2267
semicircular canals, 2313
see also hearing, noise
Easthaugh, Cyril (Bishop of Peterborough),
 348
Eastwood, Clint, 1898
eating,
compulsive, 1188
at dinner party, 2662-6
Ebbinghaus, Hermann, 1828
Eccles, John Carew, 1828

chiasma, 1615
ciliary muscles in, 1617
compound, 1658
cone of, 1703
conjugate movements of, 1703
conjunctiva, 1703
    conjunctival reflex, 1703
convergence of, 1705
cornea, 1705
    corneal reflection, 1705
    corneal reflex, 1705
corresponding points in, 1706
description of, 1885
exophthalmic goiter and, 1884
extrinsic eye muscles, 1885
forea, 1948
glaucoma, 1978
iris, 2073
lens accommodation, 1345
mirror of emotion, 463
postrotational nystagmus, 2217
pupil, 2247
resolving power of, 2265
retina, 2265
    blind spot of, 1548
    retinal rivalry, 2265-6
training of, 462
working of the, 459-62, *410*
see also body, vision
Eysenck, Prof. Hans,
antisocial behavior, 2118, 2119
clairvoyance, 688
homosexuality, 1149
on IQ, 611, 655, 677, 680
personality types, 2551
physical attraction, 72
psychiatry, 1517, 2515
on psychoanalysis, 720

F *Face of the Third Reich, The* (Joachim C. Fest), 1457
facilitation, social, 2339
Faerie Queene (Spenser), 900
Fairbairn, Dr. W. R., 926-7
Faith, Adam, 1943
faith healing, 257, 258, 454, 666
commission's report on, 814-15
definition of, 1040, 1908
forms of, 815-16
origins of, 734, 738
and orthodox medicine, 817
working of, 1040-41
see also acupuncture etc.
family,
definition of, 1908
effect on child of, 1468-71
first group experience, 2819, 2820
function of, 1374-8, 1631-3
nuclear,
    dangers of, 2821
    growth of, 441-2, 2150
one-parent, 2325-8
problem, 1633-6
structure of, 1334-8
    cultural variations in, 1836-40
Family and Marriage in Britain, The (Dr. Ronald Fletcher), 1952
fanaticism, 1908
fantasy, 1908
sexual, 2054-7
and social adjustment, 2452
Farmer, Dr. Mary, 1378
Farmer's Allminax (Josh Billings), 1291
fashion, and sexual attraction, 1716-20
see also appearance, clothes
Fast, Dr. Julius, on body language, 1090, 1132, 1134
fatalism, 1908
father,
figure, 1908-9
fixation, 1909
changing role of, 1975-7
see also family

fatigue, 1909
driver, 1867, *1866*
pilot, 1863-5
Fay, Janet, 1712
fear,
in animals, 861
cause of harm, 886
definition of, 859, 1909
eliminating, 960
incidence of, 859-60
inherited, 887
measurement of, 861
natural response, 861
physiology of, 859, 860
pleasurable, 886-7
psychological signs of, 860
Fear of Flying (Erica Jong), 1302
Fearn, Donald, and sadistic murder, 1594
Fechner, Gustav, 1909
Fechner's paradox, 1909
Federov, Nikolai, 431, 433
feedback, 1909
negative, 2148
fellatio, 1909
see also sex
Feldmesser, Robert, on capitalism, 2476
Feminine Mystique, The (Betty Friedan), 1522, 2726
Feminine Psychology (Karen Horney), 1954, 2685
Fernandez, Raymond, 1712, 1715
Fernel, Jean, 303
fertility,
definition of, 919-20
male, 921-3
    see also impotence
tests for, 923
Fest, Joachim C., 1457, 1458
fetishism, 291, 1910
definition of, 1910
Krafft-Ebing on, 501
as male prerogative, 778-82
see also sexual deviation
Firebrace, Brig. R. C., 1306
Fisher, Seymour,
on orgasm, 1888
on sexual monotony, 1315
fishing,
fish breeding, 2562-4
and food shortage, 2561-2
see also food
Fishlock, David, on technology, 2318

fixation, 1910-11
see also father fixation
flagellation, 1911
see also sexual deviation
Flammarion, Camille, 755
Fleming, Sir Alexander, and penicillin, 1407, 2419, *2421*
Flesh of the Gods (Douglas Sharon), 216
Fletcher, Dr. James (NASA administrator), 2658
Fletcher, Dr. Ronald,
family rights, 1378
role swapping, 1952
flirtation,
art of, 1025-6
body language in, 1026
reasons for, 1026-8
compare titillation, 617
see also love
flocillation, 1911
fluoridation, opposition to, 2616-17
flying,
fear of, 1768, 1770-72
love of, 1768-70
pilot fatigue, 1863
flying saucer, *see* Unidentified Flying Objects (UFO),
Flying Saucers Have Landed (Leslie and Adamski), 2556
Flynn, Errol, as sex symbol, 1875
Folk, Carl, 1594, *1595*
food,
balanced diet, 1057
body's use of, 1056-7, 1108
calories, 1189, 90
caries, 1588
carbohydrate, 1057-8, 1110
    starch, 1059
    sugar, 1059
catabolism of, 1588
definition of, 1056
drink, 1059
and energy, 1110
and the environment, 2233-4, *2235*
fats, 1058, 1110
fishing's contribution to, 2561
minerals in, 1147
most useful, 1059
need for, 1056
protein, 1057, 1108-10
    milk, 1058-9
shortage of, 2537-41
and slimming, 1190

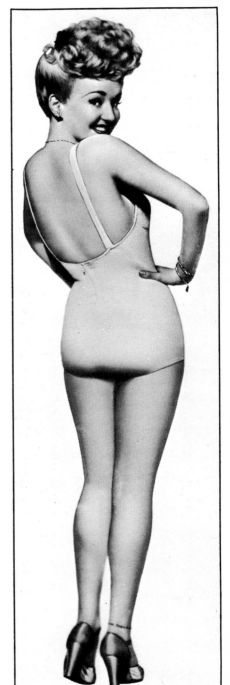

Kobal Collection

GUIDE TO VOLUMES

Volume	Pages	Volume	Pages	Volume	Pages
One	7–120	Nine	967–1080	Seventeen	1927–2040
Two	127–240	Ten	1087–1200	Eighteen	2047–2160
Three	247–360	Eleven	1207–1320	Nineteen	2167–2280
Four	367–480	Twelve	1327–1440	Twenty	2287–2400
Five	487–600	Thirteen	1447–1560	Twenty-one	2407–2520
Six	607–720	Fourteen	1567–1680	Twenty-two	2527–2640
Seven	727–840	Fifteen	1687–1800	Twenty-three	2647–2760
Eight	847–960	Sixteen	1807–1920	Twenty-four	2767–2880

KEY TO INDEX

Major entries are in bold type and minor entries in light type. To find a reference first locate it under its first letter (e.g. s for **sex**). Entries are sometimes subdivided (e.g. **sex**, enjoyment of, 2370-73). A *see also* italic entry indicates additional information. Major book, film and play entries are in ***bold italics***. Major book entries appear as follows—e.g. ***Unknown Self, The*** (George Groddeck), 258. *Italic* page number entries mean a picture.

immaturity, in bachelor, 435
immortality, and religion, 2063
see also after life
immunization,
definition of, 2027
growth of, 2448
and infant mortality, 1267-9
Imperial Animal, The (Fox and Tiger), 648, 970
impotence, 217-18, 343-6
definition of, 2027
erectio deficiens, 1857
in middle age, 1047
and neurosis, 889
see also sex
imprinting, 2027
imprisonment,
costs of, 1141
public attitudes to, 1140
reforms in, 1141, 1143
see also criminal, prison
infertility,
diagnosing, 946-7
folklore surrounding, 950
treatment of, 947-9
inbreeding, 2027
Inaudible Becomes Audible, The (Konstantin Raudive), 1307
incest,
definition of, 2027
in dreams, 17, 2027-8
secret desire for, 270
taboos, 232-3, 1649
incompatability, sexual, 1694-7
see also marriage, sex
incontinence, 2028
incubator, advantages of, 1135-6
induction, sympathetic, 2366
industry, women in, 1760
inertia, 2028
infantilism, 2028
Infants and Mothers (Dr. Berry Brazelton), 1623

infection, and cleanliness, 2049
inferiority complex, 2028
see also complex, personality
infidelity,
incidence of, 369
reasons for, 370-73
see also adultery, love, marriage
Infinite Hive, The (Rosalind Heywood), 756
influence,
of advertising, 2571-2
effects of others', 2569, 2572
entertainment idols, 2570
personal, 2573
of political leaders, 2569-70
information,
overload in driving, 1809-12
theory, 2028-9
inhibition,
definition of, 2029
internal, 2030
proactive, 2218
sexual, 1773-6
see also frigidity
initiation rite, 2029
initiative, leading to dominance, 112
Inkeles, Alex, and class structure, 2478
insanity,
cacodemonia in, 1551
caused by drugs, 552-3
and the criminal, 1738-41
difficulty in diagnosing, 938-40
and lobotomy, 166
see also mental handicap, mental health
insect, clock mechanism in, 133
insecurity,
foster-child delusion, 1948
see also child
leading to jealousy, 199
motivating boss figure, 181, 182, 184
tests of, 2850
insemination, artificial, effects of, 2447-8

insight, 2029
therapy, 2029
insomnia, 2029
ahypnosia, 1364
see also sleep
instinct,
and basic need, 1490
complementary, 1657
component, 1658
definition of, 2029-30
and shamanism, 206, 207
and sixth sense, 190
integration, racial, 1763
Integrative Action of the Nervous System, The (Charles Sherrington), 302
intelligence,
adult, 1362
and age, 507
in animals, 455-7
and appearance, 458
and artistic ability, 508-9
average, 406
and brain structure, 458
change in, 656
in children, 428
definition of, 405-6, 2030
effects of drugs on, 458, 508
effect of motivation on, 407
factors affecting, 407
heredity, 425, 610-11
physical factors, 508
social factors, 654-5
and happiness, 407
highest recorded, 427
idiot savant, 2027
increase in, 508, 509, 657
intelligence quotient (IQ), tests of, 101, 406, 612-13, 653
and age, 406
ball and field test, 1490
beta test, 1512
comprehension test, 1658
definition of, 407, 2030, 2073
designing, 84, 611
fables test, 1908
function of, 406
G. factor in, 1949
original thinking and, 654, 695
validity of, 653
late development of, 655
in machine, 426
and mental illness, 428, 457, 509
originality of, 654
and physical activity, 509
racial differences in, 426, 677-80
sex difference in, 83, 426
and sexual behavior, 2321-4
study of, 457-8
and versatility of adjustment, 609
Interpretation of Dreams, The (Sigmund Freud), 717
interview,
conducting, 2277
depth, 1781
halo effect, 1980
interviewer bias, 2072
stress in, 2342
techniques for success in, 1193
introspection, 2072
introversion, 54-8
definition of, 2072
sexual preferences of introvert, 72
see also personality
intuition,
definition of, 2072
developing, 2160
attempt to mechanize, 166
Invisibles, The (Francis Huxley), 503
Ipomea cairica (Morning Glory), as drug, 215, *213*
Irons, Cap. Barry, 349-50
irritability, 2073
Irvine, William, 220, 222

B.B.C./Ardea/Picturepoint

Leek, Sybil, 578-9
Leftwich, Norman (dowser), 1172-3
Lehman, H. C. on middle-age crisis, 1997
leisure,
and automation, 1524-5, 1542-6
effects of increased, 1524-8
Lenin, Nikolai,
and the Cheka, 2383
and revolution, 1531
Leonski, Joseph, 1713
Leopold, Nathan, 1711-12
lesbianism,
development of, 1126-7
incidence of, 1125
problems of, 1128
recognition of, 1127
see also homosexuality, sex
Leslie, David, on flying saucers, 2556
letter writing, hints on, 658
Levi-Strauss, Claude, kinship studies, 1338
Leviathan (Thomas Hobbes), 975
Levinson, Boris M., on pets, 2742, 2743
levitation, 2075
and Daniel Dunglass Home, 1123-4, 1153-4
Gasparin's experiments, 1153
Levy, Dr. David (psychiatric theorist), 1792
liar, compulsive
character of, 623-5
pathological, 2194
liberty, and police state, 2383-7
libido, 2075
Lichtenstein, Roy, 2671
lie detector, 2074
Liebeault, Dr. A. A., on mesmerism, 895-6
light,
angstrom unit, 1387
diffraction of, 1782
idioretinal, 2027
Lincoln, Abraham, 981
Lind, James, on scurvy, 2223-4

Lindemann, Dr. Hanse, 518-19
Linder, D., 90
Listening with the Third Ear (T. Reik), 2826
Littrow, Joseph von, 1064
Lloyd Morgan, C., 457
lobotomy, 166
damage resulting from, 1010-11
frontal, 1948
validity of, 1010
see also brain
Locke, John,
on conscience, 2500
on phobia, 2612
Lodge, Sir Oliver, 356, *357*
telepathy test, 786
Loeb, Richard, 1711-12
Loellgen, Herbert, on kissing, 901
logic, 239-40
training in, 479
Lolita (Nabokov), 1453
loner, character of the, 833-7
Long, Max Freedom, 1107
Longford, Lord, on pornography, 660
Longmore, Donald (research physiologist), 1412
Loon, Hendrik Willem van, 392
Loren, Sophia, 89
Lorenz, Konrad,
on aggression, 40, 630
bereavment, 2275
imprint experiment, 104
mood convection, 878
on sport, 681-3
love,
attracting men, 1319
conceptions of, 2628-9
courtship behavior, 139, 1706
derivation of, 87-8
falling in, 103
first, 1262

and friendship, 1117, 2723-4
and insecurity, 2630
learning to, 2630-31
memory of past, 2033-5
in middle age, 820-24
mother, 103-4, *105*
neurotic components of, 1159-60
multiple, 1339-43
parental, 1116
romantic, 465-8
development of, 92
need for, 413-18
selfish emotion, 89
and the teenager, 748-52
unrequited, 941
see also marriage, sex
Love Story (Erich Segal), 2736-7
Love and Will (Dr. Rollo May), 1430, 1870
Loved One, The (Evelyn Waugh), 2743
Lovell, K., on gifted children, 862
loyalty, within marriage, 2682-3
LSD, *see* lysergic acid diethylamide
luck, and actors, 315-17
Lueger, Dr. Karl, on antisemitism, 1787
Lull, Ramon, and robots, 2704-5
Luria, Alexander, 282, 283-4
and brain damage, 445
Lurie, Alison, 1047
Lyell, Sir Charles, 222, 225
lysergic acid diethylamide (LSD),
effects of, 409, 531, 554
and perception, 408
use in psychotherapy, 110
see also drugs

M

Macdougall, Prof. William, 454
and telepathy, 786, 1063
MacEwen, W., on bone tissue transplant, 1392
machine,
disadvantages of, 2316
effects of, 1660-64
and medicine, 1135-9
see also automation, robot
MacKenzie, Andrew, 401, 402
Macklin, Charles, 315-16
MacNeice, Louis, 935
Maddison, Dr. John, 2061
Magee, Bryan, 1125
Magic Island (William Seabrook), 503
magnetism, possible healing force of, 895, 896
make-up, and physical attractiveness, 103
see also appearance, beauty
Making of the English Working Classes, The (E. P. Thompson), 440
Malachy, St., 982
Male and Female (Margaret Mead), 1674
malnutrition,
cause of, 1147
and food aid, 2538-9
incidence of, 2538
see also dieting, food
Malthus, Rev. Thomas, 745, 813
population explosion, 2180
Mamelles de Tirésias, Les (G.Apollinaire), 2755
Man and his Symbols (Carl Jung), 96
Man on his Nature (Charles Sherrington), 303
Man's Presumptuous Brain (A. T. W. Simeons), 190
mandragora, as aphrodisiac, 1748
mandrake, *258*
mania,
collecting, 1643
processomania, 2218
religious, 2265
wandering, 2395
manic-depression, 671
cyclothymia, 1728
intermission during, 2030
see also psychosis, psychotherapy
Manning, Matthew, on the brain rhythm, 2133
Mansfield, Sir James, and criminal insanity, 1739

Marshall Cavendish

training, 286-9
visual, 282-5, 288
see also brain, learning
Memory (Ian Hunter), 276
Men at Work (Stuart Chase), 1833
Mendel, Gregor, and discovery of genetics, 1029-30
menopause, 1614
effect on sex life, 218
physiology of, 1515-18
symptoms, 1537
treatment for, 1538-40
menstruation, 1385
premenstrual tension, 2217-18
in puberty, 1964
and sex,
   sexual behavior, 218
   sexual response, 120
mental handicap,
amentia and, 1385
autism and, 1489
in children, 1308-11
cretinism, 1726
mongolism, 2127
mental health,
genetics and, 2460-1
lead poisoning and, 2459-60
mentalism, 2125
mental set, 2125
menticide, 2125
see also brainwashing
Menuhin, Yehudi, childhood genius of, 698, 863
meprobamate, 2125
Mercader, Ramon, and Trotsky's death, 1713, *1714*
Meredith, James, 1767
Mermet, Abbé, 897
and radiesthesia, 1104
Merrylees, Col. K. W. (dowser), 1173
mescaline, 2125
see also drugs
Mesmer, Franz, 296, 298, 666, *297*
faith healing methods, 736
mesmerism, 894-5
   see also hypnotism
mesmerism,
developments from, 896-7
technique of, 894-5, 2125
see also hypnotism
mesomorph, 162, 2125
and athletic performance, 2290-91
metabolism, 2125
metamphetamine, 2125
see also drugs
metaphysics, 2125
metapsychology, 2125
metazoa, 2125
methadone, 2125
methodology, 2125
metonymy, 2125
Metraux, Alfred, on voodoo, 503, 504, 506, 597
metrazul, 2125
Michelet, Jules, 2137
microcephaly, 2125
microphobia, 2126
see also phobia
micropsia, 2126
microtome, 2126
middle age,
affairs in, 1046-51
problems of, 1996-9
stress in, 2023-6
see also age
migraine, 2126
Milgram, Dr. S., experiments on influence, 2572
militarism, history of, 999-1003
Mill, John Stuart, 2126
on contraception, 746, 747
high intelligence of, 427, 863
on punishment, 1097
Miller, Alan, 90
Miller, Prof, Henry, on euthanasia, 1368

Miller, Dr. J. G., driving techniques, 1812
Miller, Dr. Neal, on placebo, 1257
Million and One Nights, A (Terry Ramsaye), 1894
Mills, Hayley, *236*
Mills, C. Wright.
and New Left, 2303
on protest, 2335
Milner, Brenda, 281
mimetic response, 2126
mind, 2126
ambivalence in, 1385
censor in, 1590
expansion of, 2518
mind-body problem, 2126
mind-muscle co-ordination, 1551
see also brain, memory
Mind of Man, The (Nigel Calder), 2654
Mind over Matter (Louisa Rhine), 1154
Mind of a Mnemonist (Alexander Luria), 282
Mind Possessed, The (William Sargant), 528
mind reading, see telepathy
minerals, essential in diet, 1147
miosis, 2127
mirror writing, 2127
misanthrope, 2127
miscegenation, 2127
see also marriage
misogyny,
in literature, 1499-1500
in primitive tribes, 1497-8
misopedic, 2127
mistress, character of, 369, 489-92
see also adultery, infidelity, love
Mitchell, Juliet, 2729
Mitford, Nancy, 319
mitochondria, 2127
mitosis, 2127
mixoscopia, 2127
mnemonic devices, 288, 289, 2127
see also memory
mobility,
and future shock, 2843-4
vertical, 2394
Modes of Social Ascent Through Education (Ralph H. Turner), 2496
molar behavior, 2127
molecular behavior, 2127
Molina, Tirso de, 511
Mompesson, John, 627-8
monadism, 2127
Mondrian, Piet, 212, *211*
Mondrone, Father Domenico, 323
money,
changes life-style, 1904-7
need for, 1877-81
mongolism, 2127
monism, 2127
Moniz, Antonio, and psychosurgery, 1010
Moniz, Egas, 166
monomania, 2127
Monroe, Marilyn, 389, 1875, *1874*
cosmetic surgery on, 2412, *2413*
Monstrous Regiment of Women, The (John Knox), 1499
moon, effect on behavior, 1008
moon illusion, 2128
Moore, Archie, *683*
Moorhouse, Geoffrey, 517
morality,
of abortion, 2812
sexual, 2809-12
sphincter, 2341
Moreau, Gustave, 2752
Moreno, Jacob, and psychodrama, 839
Morgan, Patricia, on feral man, 2820, 2821
morphine, 2128
see also drugs
morphology, 2128
Morris, Desmond, 28
on aggression, 40
anthropomorphism, 2743
on gifted apes, 863

male supremacy, 1951
mobile territory, 1576
pair bonding, 1313
sense of smell, 593
on sexual attraction, 70
status sex, 1578
Morris, Jan (James), on transsexuality, 1178
Morris, Dr. Robert, on precognition, 1227
mortality, infant, 1267
mortido, 2128
Mortimer, Robert, Bishop of Exeter, 348
Moss, Dr. Peter, on hysteria, 880
mother,
adaptation to motherhood, 1890-93
complex, 2128
love of child for, 1484-6, *1487*
maternal instinct, 1519-21
maternal role, 1491-3
surrogate, 2128
working, 1758-62
see also child, family, marriage
Mothers, The (Briffaut), 178
motivation, 2128
effect on intelligence, 407
extrinsic, 1885
intrinsic, 2072
motor skills,
and memory, 274, 277
sharpening, 808
motor strip, 163, *165*
see also brain
Mountbatten, Lord Louis, 135
mourning, 2143-6, 2274-5, *2147*
in child, 2275
manifestation of, 2273-5
see also death
Muggeridge, Malcolm, on television, 1388
muller-lyer illusion, 2128
multiple choice technique, 2128
multiple sclerosis, 447, 1783, 2128
Mumford, Lewis, on Roman building style, 2426
murder, reasons for, 1711-15
murderer, character of, 1711-15
Murray, Gilbert, 757
Murray, Dr. Margaret, 576
Murray, Dr. R. H., 400
muscle, reading, 2129
see also body
music,
absolute pitch in, 1345
appreciating, 1194
and the ear, 528
history of, 1991-5
popular,
   The Beatles, 1968-9, *1970*
   and youth, 1939-43
mutation, 2129
My Life (Havelock Ellis), 353
myasthenia, 2129
myelin, 2129
Myers, F. W. H., 190, 664
myograph, 2129
mysophobia, 2129
see also phobia
Myth of Mental Illness, The (Thomas Szasz), 939
Myths and Mythmakers (Prof. Fiske), 1171
myxedema, 2129

N **Napier, Sir Charles,** 915
Napier, John, *1752*
narcissism, 386-90, 2129
narcoanalysis, 2129
narcolepsy, 2129
narcotics, working of, 574, 2129
see also drugs, *and under separate entries*
National Labor Relations (Wagner) Act (1935), 1701
nationalism,
cause of war, 1003
rise of, 1022-4
nativism, 2129
see also heredity

KEY TO INDEX

Major entries are in bold type and minor entries in light type. To find a reference first locate it under its first letter (e.g. s for **sex**). Entries are sometimes subdivided (e.g. **sex**, enjoyment of, 2370-73). A *see also* italic entry indicates additional information. Major book, film and play entries are in ***bold italics***. Major book entries appear as follows—e.g. ***Unknown Self, The*** (George Groddeck), 258. *Italic* page number entries mean a picture.

paralysis,
cerebral palsy, 1614
diplegia, 1782
hemiplegia, 2004
paranoia,
definition of, 2192
eccentric, 1828
nagging wife, 228-30
paranormal phenomena, *see* supernatural
parapsychology, 356, 2192-3
aura in, 1488
cross-correspondence in, 1726-7
see also extrasensory perception, supernatural
Parapsychology (John Gaither Pratt), 626, 756
parathymia, 2193
parent,
and child's upbringing, 2237-40
effect of lack of parent, 2325-8
influence on child's relationships, 1959-62
substitute, 90
see also family, marriage
Parhon, Prof. C. I., 2060
Parkinson, Prof. C. Northcote, 2379-82
Parkinson's Law, 2379-81
injelitis, 2381-2
Parkinson's Disease, 447, 2193
and stereotoxic surgery, 1011
Parsons, Talcott (sociologist), 2431
partner,
choice of, 87
opposites theory, 88-90
parental substitute, 90
similarity theory, 88
see also love, marriage
passivity, 2193
in marriage, 1475-8
Pasteur, Louis,
on disease, 2050, 2051
lateral thinking, 1558
patriarchy, 2194
Patterns in Forcible Rape (Dr. Menachem Amir), 2749
patriotism,
and nationalism, 1021-4
perverted, 1020-21, 1023-4
see also nationalism
Paul VI, Pope, 323-4, 327, 348, 811
Pauling, Linus, 1146
Pavlov, Ivan, 93, 185, 2194
conditioned reflex, 274, 328-30, 419
internal inhibition, 2030
see also reflex
peacemaking, qualities required for, 840
Pearson, Karl, and statistics, 2194
pecking order,
in hens, 111
human, 114
need for, 2194
see also dominance
Peckinpah, Sam, 1862
pederasty, 203, 2194
see also homosexuality
pedophilia,
definition of, 2194
incidence of, 1449, 1452, 1453
peer group, 2194
Peking man (sinanthropus), 2194, 2338
Pemberton Billing, Noel, and sex in theatre, 1370
Penfield Wilder, 158, 163, 164, 166, 173
and memory, 285, 1911
penicillin, resistance to, 2418-20
see also drugs
penis envy, 2194
pentothal, 2194
perception,
and apparent movement, 1408
creative, 391-4
definition of, 2195
depth, 1781
and distortion, 408-12
personal interpretation of, 761-5
prägnanz, 2217

time, 2195
subliminal, 2342
visual, 2394
see also imagination, vision
perfume,
history of, 2480-81, 2483
manufacture of, 2482-3
reasons for using, 2480
permissiveness,
definition of, 2195
and premarital sex, 711-12
perseveration, 2195
persistence, tests to measure, 335-6
persona, 2195
personality,
authoritarian, 1489
braggart, 898-900
cerebrotonic type of, 1614
choleric type of, 1616
comentation of, 1657
common traits in, 1657
compulsive, 1658
conation and, 1659
constitutional type of, 1704
cycloid type of, 1728
definition of, 2195
dionysian side of, 1782
disorders, 2195
dual, 1828
see also multiple personality
Electra complex and, 1830
gauging, 2400, 2484
inadequacy of, 2027
inkblot (Rorschach) test on, 2029, 2266
integrated, 2030
internalization of, 2030
introjection of, 2072
multiple, 2128
coconsciousness in, 1642-3
oral type, 2152
overdirective, 2638
typing, 2195
Personality Changes (P. W. Tow), 1010
persuasion, acquiring art of, 359-60
perversion, 2214

see also sexual perversion
pessomancy, 936
pets,
benefit to children, 2742
consolation from, 2742
history of, 2741
human attitude to, 2739, 2741, 2743, *2740*
Peter, Dr. Laurence J., 2379, 2382
Peter Principle, 2379
Petitpierre, Dom Robert, 350
peyotl, 215
see also drugs
phagomania, 2214
phallic mother, theory of, 250
phallic stage, in infancy, 33, 2214
phantasm, 2214
see also supernatural
Phantasms of the Living (Gurney, Myers and Podmore), 664
phantom limb, 2214
pharmacology, 2214
phengophobia, 2214
see also phobia
phenomena, spontaneous, 2341
phenomenology, 2214
Philadelphia Association, 858
Philip II of Spain, 1501, *1502*
phobia,
aerophobia, 1771-2
cause of, 2613
in children, 888
cure for, 912-13, 2614
behavioral approach to, 913
psychotherapy, 110
social approach to, 913
definition of, 887, 2214, 2610-11
diagnosing, 913
history of, 2612
incidence of, 887-8
major neurosis, 671
most common, 888, 911-12, 2610, 2612, 2613
theory of, 911, 2611-12
phonophobia, 2214
see also phobia
phrenology, 161, 935, 2215, *162*

Marshall Cavendish

Barnaby's

GUIDE TO VOLUMES

Volume	Pages	Volume	Pages	Volume	Pages
One	7–120	Nine	967–1080	Seventeen	1927–2040
Two	127–240	Ten	1087–1200	Eighteen	2047–2160
Three	247–360	Eleven	1207–1320	Nineteen	2167–2280
Four	367–480	Twelve	1327–1440	Twenty	2287–2400
Five	487–600	Thirteen	1447–1560	Twenty-one	2407–2520
Six	607–720	Fourteen	1567–1680	Twenty-two	2527–2640
Seven	727–840	Fifteen	1687–1800	Twenty-three	2647–2760
Eight	847–960	Sixteen	1807–1920	Twenty-four	2767–2880

KEY TO INDEX

Major entries are in bold type and minor entries in light type. To find a reference first locate it under its first letter (e.g. s for **sex**). Entries are sometimes subdivided (e.g. **sex**, enjoyment of, 2370-73). A *see also* italic entry indicates additional information. Major book, film and play entries are in **bold italics**. Major book entries appear as follows—e.g. ***Unknown Self, The*** (George Groddeck), 258. *Italic* page number entries mean a picture.

Kobal Collection

types of, 1606-9
VD clinics, 1628-30
Venus in Furs (Leopold von Sacher-Masoch), 312
verbal skill, female superiority in, 85, 86
see also speech
verbalism, 2393-4
Vernon, J. A. on sensory deprivation, 740
Victoria, Queen, and emancipation, 767, 769
Vidor, King, 1826
Vinci, Leonardo da, 212
Vindication of the Rights of Women (Mary Wollstonecraft), 767
violence,
in entertainment, 1294
in marriage, 2582
resulting from pornography, 663
in urban environment, 1465
virginity, society's attitude to, 1379-83
virilism, 2394
viscerotonia, 2394
vision,
afterimage, 1363
and age, 800, 2815-16
ambiguous figure, 1385, 2148
amblyopia, 1385
apparition, 1408
astigmatism, 1474
autokinetic effect, 1489
in babies, 799
Bidwell's ghost (Purkinje afterimage), 1513, 2247
brightness of, 1550-51
central, 1590
chromatic aberration of, 1617
and color, 800
see also color blindness
critical flicker fusion (CFF), 1726
dark adaptation, 1728
day blindness, 1728
definition of, 2394

diplopia, 1782
far-sightedness, 1908
figural aftereffect, 1910
figure-ground phenomenon, 1910
flight of colors, 1911
geometrical illusion, 1950
and hearing, 800
hemianopia of, 2004
and illusion, 1899-1903
imperfect, 462-3
indirect, 2028
Landolt circles test of, 2074
object blindness, 2150
photopic, 2215
peripheral, 2195
positive afterimage, 2216-17
sensitivity of, 799-800
transmission of, 460
tunnel, 2369
visual acuity, 2394
visual logic, tests for, 67-8
visual perception, and depth, 81-2
vitalism, 2395
vitamins,
definition of, 1144
effect of overdose, 1146-7
most useful, 1144
  A, 1145
  B, 1145
  C, 1145-6
  D, 1146
  E, 1146
  K, 1146
need for, 1144-5
pills, 1146
vocabulary, tests of, 116
see also speech
vocational guidance, 2395
see also job
Vogel, Dr. Marcel, 789
Vogt, Evon, 1172

Volin, Michael, on yoga, 2654, 2656
voodoo, 503-6
ceremony of, 597
hierarchy of, 594
  guédé of, 596, 598
  loa of, 594-6
Voodoo Gods (Zora Houston), 503
Voodoo in Haiti (Alfred Metraux), 503
voyeurism,
character of voyeur, 1098-1100, 2395
psychological reasons for, 1100-1101
as substitute, 1314
victims of, 1102

W

Wagner, Dr. Nathaniel, on physiology of sex, 905
Wakley, Thomas, founder of *The Lancet*, 896
Walden Two (B.F. Skinner), 421
Walker, Benjamin, 2114
Walker, Kenneth, 868, 871, 902
Wallace, Alfred Russell, 222, 356, *357*
Wallace, George, 2347
Walster, Elaine, 69
on social intercourse, 2652
Wangensteen, Dr. Owen, 1395
war,
and aggression, 45-8
biological weapons in, 2583-5
chemical weapons, 2584
and commercial gain, 1053-4
games, 1055
loyalty in, 1002-3
lure of, 1003
nuclear weapons, 2585
and pacifism, 1054-5
psychological, 2247
responsibility in, 1052-3
tradition of, 999, 1001, *1000*
warrior caste, 1001-2
see also aggression, conflict
War Between the Tates, The (Alison Lurie), 1047
War Without Weapons (Philip Goodhard and Christopher Chataway), 683
Warhol, Andy and good taste, 2671
Warr, George de la, 1107, 1306, *1305*
Warrant for Genocide (Norman Colin), 1787
Washburn, S.L., 40
Washington, George, on disease, 2050
Wasson, R.G., 216
water, as dream symbol, 20, 22
see also symbol
Water-witching USA (Evon Vogt and Ray Hyman), 1172
Watergate affair, 1329-30, 1331
Watkins, Anita, 1063
Watkins, Graham, 1063
Watson, John B.,
behaviorism, 1659
environmental programing, 1581, 2395
habit training, 2240
on phobia, 888
Watson, Lyall, 190, 755, 756, 816
effect of moon on behavior, 1749
evolution in animals, 1061
telepathy, 787
thoughtography, 1307
Watts, Charles, 795-6
Waugh, Evelyn, 2743
Wayne, Ricky, on bodybuilding, 2734
Weber, Max, on status, 2495
  Weber's law, 2395
Wechsler, David, on intelligence tests, 2395
Welch, Leslie, 287, 288
Wells, Charles Deville, 932
Wertheimer, Max, 2395
Wesley, John, 877
Wesolowski, W., 2431
West, John Anthony, 1006, 1007
West, Mae, 1875
and censorship, 2263
Westlake, Dr. Aubrey, 1107

Color Library International

GUIDE TO VOLUMES

Volume	Pages	Volume	Pages	Volume	Pages
One	7–120	Nine	967–1080	Seventeen	1927–2040
Two	127–240	Ten	1087–1200	Eighteen	2047–2160
Three	247–360	Eleven	1207–1320	Nineteen	2167–2280
Four	367–480	Twelve	1327–1440	Twenty	2287–2400
Five	487–600	Thirteen	1447–1560	Twenty-one	2407–2520
Six	607–720	Fourteen	1567–1680	Twenty-two	2527–2640
Seven	727–840	Fifteen	1687–1800	Twenty-three	2647–2760
Eight	847–960	Sixteen	1807–1920	Twenty-four	2767–2880

KEY TO INDEX

Major entries are in bold type and minor entries in light type. To find a reference first locate it under its first letter (e.g. s for **sex**). Entries are sometimes subdivided (e.g. **sex**, enjoyment of, 2370-73). A *see also* italic entry indicates additional information. Major book, film and play entries are in ***bold italics***. Major book entries appear as follows—e.g. ***Unknown Self, The*** (George Groddeck), 258. *Italic* page number entries mean a picture.

CONTRIBUTORS

The following is a list of the writers who have contributed articles to *Understanding Human Behavior*.
Tony Aldous
Jane Alexander
Bill Breckon
Sandy Brown
John H. Clark
F. J. Ebling
Humphrey Evans
Jerry Fox
Judy Froshaug
John Gay
Simon Goodenough
Martin Herbert
Alan Hughes
Maggie Ing
Paul Kline
Andrew Mayes
Caroline Moorehead
Jeremy Pascall
Michael Prideaux
James Reason
Caroline Richards
Ursula Robertshaw
John Scott
Frank Smyth
Peter Spence
John Stevenson
Peter Sylvester
Penny Vincenzi
Brian Ward
Geoff Watts
Arline Whittaker
Glenn Wilson

U.P.I.